Feel The Mind, Touch The Heart

Sara Jo Bowling

ArLu Publishing

Feel the Mind, Touch the Heart
Published by ArLu Publishing
Salem, AR

ISBN: 979-8-218-23268-9

AUTOBIOGRAPHY / Personal Memoirs

Cover design by Natasha Brown. All rights reserved by author.

QUANTITY PURCHASES: Schools, companies, professional groups, clubs, and other organizations may qualify for special terms when ordering quantities of this title. For information, email sarabowling55@gmail.com.

Printed in the United States of America.

ArLu Publishing

To You, My Readers

When publishing "Feel The Mind, Touch The Heart"
for the second time, I considered corrections. Yet,
the more I pondered the idea…the more I thought it
necessary to leave as written.

I am the author, editor and proofer. This book is
where I was, at the time. The content, solid.

As I groveled to some, their response was lack of
concern to my imperfection. Huh! How about that?!

I hope the part of my journey contained in this book,
to be of benefit for those who read.

Sara

Introduction

Dear Readers,

This book is a compilation of writings, most of which span the years of 2013, 2014 and early 2015. In retrospect, during that time I was continually experiencing mild mania. At times I was aware of my elevated mood, at other times I wasn't. Regardless, very little sleep occurred during that time…to the point I could feel myself physically deteriorating. In March of 2015 I was hospitalized for a month. During that time I started a new drug regimen which has tremendously improved my life. The contents of this book are not in chronological order until the writing "Reddish-Orange". Those are post hospital works from Spring 2015 to mid 2017. Very little writing has occurred since the hospitalization. I guess this whole book was a catharsis. One can note resolve towards the end of the book. Also included in this book are some writings from the early 1990's. Those writings are dated. I began writing posts on Facebook and many of my friends encouraged me to blog or publish. I have a blogsite, alas I never really understood the blogging world. I'm old-fashioned! But I figured out enough to be able to post my blog writings for my Facebook friends. They were my sounding board. Even though I didn't ask for their permission! Ha! My writing appears in "block form". When I was zoned into what I was writing, I disregarded paragraphs, etc. It's as if the words were just "jumping out". I was only concentrating on the content. I apologize to all my English teachers from grade school through college!! Also, I want to be totally honest. When reading over the contents, I realized how much I spoke of the "spiritual". But if you want a record of my Sunday School attendance...well, I could do much better. The bed is so comfortable on Sunday mornings!

I want to thank all the mental health professionals... doctors, nurses, therapists, social workers, and aides that have helped me throughout my lifetime. Much gratitude to an exceptional physician who humanely administered beneficial ECTs. Special thanks to the workers "behind the scenes" at hospitals and clinics. I am forever indebted to all of you, for your patience, compassion, knowledge, dedication and hard work. Also, "thank you" to the clergy who have been instrumental in my life. Your devotion to your "calling" continues to benefit me. (Especially grateful for Bro. Ray) To my family and friends...You're The Best! I love you! (Some of you "made this book happen" literally...Some of you "saved my skin" literally.) And God...THANK YOU! With warm regards to all, Sara.

This book is dedicated to Momma and Daddy.

In memory of Delores and Evelyn. Much Peace.

Survival – the ability to outwit your emotions. SJB

Contents

Why Read Such "Stuff"?

Up and down. Back and forth.
So goes the writings on this tablet.
They are the facts present in this
person's life. There are no lies.

Who wants to know? Who really
cares? What does it mean to the
world? It doesn't matter. The
writer wants to express. One is
not required to read.

So, the words...they bounce "to
and fro". Why? Well, the mind
which pens the thoughts moves
vivaciously. Slow down. Stop.
No, not on your life. Relief and
freedom are the sought for result.

It can be a "ride" for the reader.
A Ferris wheel? Not always that
meek. Sometimes a roller coaster.
Possibly, it takes a bit of nerve
to board. But it might be a thrill.
Or it might make one sick.

Good and bad. Happy and sad.
These words describe the positive
drive or conflict within the author.
So, it's of a human nature? Why…
yes. Not to scare one off. On the
contrary…the writer and reader may
have something in common.

Can you relate? If so, maybe there
is shared hope. If not, maybe a
knowledge gained for future reference.
Regardless, "it is what it is". Probably
no threat of theft. Who wants such
ambivalence as a trait?

So, up and down…back and forth.
Good and bad…happy and sad.
They make up these writings.
And a warm welcome to those
who "take a look" and venture.

The Funny With The Hard

What's so funny about things being hard?
Hell...nothing! But one can experience
"funny" amongst the "hard". Thank goodness!
Did I say "joy"? Nope. Just "funny".
And that will "get you by" when you're
in the midst of crap?

Is this false? That "funny" will somehow
make the impossible possible? Well...
for me...no. In fact, many times it's
the only facet of life that makes for
survival. Save faith. But at times
faith can't be felt...and is so elusive.

And many times we need to "feel".
We need to laugh and carry-on in a
silly fashion. Make light and crazy.
Act stupid? Well, sometimes.
Although, don't confuse acting stupid
with being stupid. We can still be
intelligent while in the folly.

So, times are hard. We have a tough
road ahead of us. Shoot...We've been
walking down this particular road
for quite some time. It's getting old!
There's no end in sight. Solutions...
for the most part are very vague.
And yet we can "find funny"?

Well, if we let life play-out...
"funny" will happen. It's bound to.
See, we are stupid. Other people are
stupid. WHAT? What a cruel thing
to say! No, no. Go back to the fact
that one can act stupid and still be
very smart.

You say you're above such simple
and insignificant behavior? I feel
sorry for you, if that's the case. It
can be fun to "act a fool". No, not
make foolish decisions with importance
being at stake. But to make people
laugh at your antics can be refreshing.
Funny to you. Funny to them.

You've had a hard day. Everything that
could go wrong, went wrong. Perhaps
ridicule was thrown at you. Self-esteem
is down for the count. You "messed-up"
big time. You get the gist...the day was
all screwed. Find "funny"? How on
earth? Yes, it's out there.

Again, let life just happen. Eventually…
instances will occur that are so insane
that the insanity will be haplessly
ridiculous. Let me clarify; the insanity
is of the carefree sense. "Care" "free".
To say, we come to the conclusion that
in the end we don't give a "rat's ass"!
And so we laugh…and it's funny.

What happens when we laugh? You know.
There's relief and release within. The "hard"
eases a bit. Things aren't so critical. We
have a reprieve from our trials. We lose
our breath not from a piercing pain…
but from gut-wrenching guffaw.

Ok…so I've stated my case. Times can
be hard and still "funny" can be found.
Humanity…being human…that's the
key. Your being. My being. It's all
that's necessary for a hilarious combustion.

Where Is The Wisdom?

Thoughts, feelings and insights bringing
a certain amount of practical knowledge.
With it come decision-making that is
beneficial to a productive and happy life.
This IS what we want...a contentment?
The arrival of joy is perhaps thought to
be associated with wisdom.

In the past, there has been the attainment
of wisdom. Obviously, not with regards
to everything...but indeed it has been
gained to a certain degree. If not...
we'd surely be "lost at sea". Yet, here
we stand on solid ground. Well...honestly,
our feet might not be planted so firmly.

Right now...at this moment, where is
the wisdom? Oh...words, how they can
deceive. That's right..."talk it up". But at
the same time recoil to an infant state of
"know-how". So, why are we at such a
loss for stability and security that is
accompanied with the wise?

Again, where does wisdom come from?
Let's see...trials, experiences, loss, gain,
exposure, pain. In other words, everyday
life. Hardships...not desirable. But at
the same time, "finding out" also comes
from the undesired. Grateful for that fact.

Maybe...just maybe we don't seem to have
much wisdom right now, because we are
experiencing the process of developing the
longed-for treasure. Could be. I think...
probably so. We are paying the price for
the rights of knowledge.

So, we go through the motions. Not in the
sense that we do not learn. No, with every
thought, feeling and experience we grow
all the more powerful. As we cry, rejoice
and hurt...we add such produced wisdom to
our individual character.

Where is the wisdom? Not too much hangin'
around right now...so it seems. Maybe it's
within reach, but we don't have the strength
to take hold. But with time...we will be able
to grab the benefits of our endurance.
And we will be blessed abundantly.

The Ball Glove

My parents. Very frugal. Yet, as a newborn I was brought home to a three-bedroom brick house with central air...newly built. They had their priorities in order. I can remember thin potato soup near the end of the month. But I always had at least one pair of Levi's 501 Button-Ups, when in high school. For many years we didn't have Christmas stockings (I guess my mother didn't think it was a necessity.) That might sound kinda mean or like too much of a "tight-wad". Who knows? I wasn't scarred. Even so, my mother kept me from physical scars...she readily took me to the dermatologist when I was a teenager. We didn't have a working television much of the time. Found out later that sometimes it was because my dad took the tube out...so we'd concentrate on our homework! That fact kinda "burned". But I always found my way to the neighbors to watch cartoons, The Brady Bunch or The Rifleman, and Perry Mason reruns. At the same time, my parents bought a fairly expensive hi-fi stereo from Brock's Audio for our family. Well enough...you get the picture. Here's "my story" for this particular blog... I was in 4th grade and the grandest thing happened. At school we received a form to fill out if we wanted to play YMCA softball!!! I was SO excited. My parents, knowing how much I loved sports, didn't have a hard time deciding to spend the money. They could see the personal investment. But there was one problem. I didn't have a ball glove. I can't really remember, but I think until then I'd always used my brothers' gloves...even though he was left-handed... opposite of me. Regardless, somehow I'd managed. But now I really needed an appropriate glove. My thought...go to Gibson's Discount Store and choose. Not to be. What then? My dad asked my brother if one of the neighbor boys had an old glove he wasn't using. Ugh!! Hopes dashed! Well, a ball glove was confiscated. Another problem presented itself. There was no "web" or "pocket" to the glove. Surely, now we'll go to Gibson's. Again...Not. What?!! To shorten the story...One night I watched as my dad sat at the dining table. He had the old, worn glove and he was sewing pieces of brown felt with strips of leather...to make a "pocket". I can see that "picture" clearly as if it was yesterday. And I cherish that vision. I wasn't too bothered by the "hand-me-down" glove. Although, in the team picture, I made sure I had my hand over the pocket part of the glove. I mean...really...what kid wouldn't? Bottom line...I could catch the ball with that glove. Wasn't that the purpose? Apparently, it affected my brother much more. As the next year he... my brother...bought me a brand new red, up-to-date glove. Nobody else had a glove of color!! And it was different...it had a hole where the index finger went. WOW...I was "hot-stuff"!! I had that glove for many, many years. But looking back...what's the memory that I hold precious? Yes, it was watching my dad take out time, and spend effort to sew a glove together...just for me! AND...He came to ALL of my games!!! I have been so blessed!

A Piece of The Pie

A fraction is what many people receive.
Bread in the Third World.
Love in the Western Continents.

Who decides the amount?
Volunteers, donations, you and me?

People cry.
A stomach not yet full.
A person so lonely, the desire to eat vanished weeks
ago.

SJB 1993

Simple Fear?

Could it be? Could it be so insignificant
that it makes one look foolish? I mean...
where are the facts? They can't be readily
identified, not to mention proven. All this
nausea. So senseless. That's it. It doesn't
make sense. What does one run from, with
such speed? Fear.

"Just do it." "Get it over with." "Take the bull by
the horns." So easily said...but. But what?
The cause. One wants to know the cause for
the apprehension. Why such insistence where
this is concerned? Well, it's thought if the
cause were to be known...appropriate action to
overcome could begin.

The answer is nowhere in sight. And it might
be some time before the least of the riddle
can be solved. So, what to do with this
churning sick stomach in the meantime?
"Oh...blow it off!" Sorry, not that easy.
I'm not you and you're not me. We may
differ in our lack of ease. No right or wrong.

The same faltering steps are taken. Yes, the same sequence of events occur. Seemingly, unable to stop the course. Driven by a radical concept of emotion. The fear is compounded and enlarged by unbridled train of thought. Why do this to oneself? Can't one see? It's all in the mind. Yes, that's where this fear lives.

So, "change your mind". "Get a fresh, new mindset." "Challenge what appears to be false beliefs." Oh...please. If it were only simple fear. There are no enemies threatening. Physical harm is not in the picture. Then what's it all about? It's the gut...where it's felt. There is a dull blade trying to make an excruciating blunt stab. It does. And then it begins to carve. Will it end?

One is stymied and stuck. Forward motion is not possible. Frozen. God have mercy! The response...trust, try again, let go of obvious "trash" that accompanies such fear. "Trash" that is possible to dispose. Practicality. How? How can logic guide when the feeling is so outrageous? One can't go it alone. There has to be a partner to fight the anxious state.

Who to ask? Where to go? Which direction to look? Well, let's see...earlier God was mentioned. Yes, there was a cry for help. Why hasn't aid been dispensed by this Being? Time? What? Again there's talk of "waiting upon the Lord"? How long? Why not now? Have to settle for the not known.

A recall...Something about looking to the hills for help to come. So, that is where I rest...on a promise. Its arrival might not be at this moment. But eventually...yes, eventually relief will make its way into my soul. Release of trials, doubts and fears. Simple fear? I think not. But a powerful source will soon crush the elusive wrath. What a welcomed and wondrous day!

Hiding Behind Glory

Wave the white flag? NO.
It's just a battle among the
war. There will be many
encounters. But try your
hardest not to lose this fight.

You're tired? Yes, I know
you are. What do you expect?
It's "tooth for tooth...
nail for nail". There is no
letting up. The enemy continues
to close in.

Ok...At least give you a break?
I guess a small respite is possible.
Yeah, you do need a chance to
regroup. You're only human.
A "shoring-up" of strength has to be.

So, you've decided not to give up?
Good for you. What made you
change your outlook? A protector?
You say you have forces coming?
And for the while you have a shield?

You now have armor? I hope so.
You are the only one left in the
bunker. What is this guard?
You say a spirit? How foolish
you are! It will not provide the
screen you need.

So, you say it will be enough to
hold the opposition at bay...
for the time being? And you claim
it's a spirit? Sounds impossible.

Well, tell me. What is "this spirit"?
It's invisible? Of course, spirits aren't
to be seen. It can also comfort?
And it's been tried and proven?
What?!! You say it's Holy?!!
Get Back!!!

Oh...Blow It Off?

I'm worrying, when I should just let it be. It's a problem I've tried to fix...but I've "missed the mark" with every attempt. And I've used many sensible methods to overcome...but to no avail. The door is hard to open. And to a degree, I've stopped trying to turn the knob. I've asked for guidance from above and sought an earthly course. But no such luck. Oh...it doesn't have anything to do with luck anyway. Ok...I'm in a quandary. Will I let the feeling of doom rule? Hell No! I'm tired of this! I don't have an answer to the problem, yet. But there is possible help on the way. I gotta keep that in mind. I can't let my apprehensive state ruin another hour. It is my time! Get Back! I say... "Mind, get out of my way!" Too much trash. Am I gonna let misery settle? Speaking of the mind...what's the deal with it anyway? I mean...I think and think. Then think some more. Digging deeper and deeper into a hole. The light gets dimmer as I sink to yet another level. But Wait! Don't give up. There's gonna be a solution. Sure enough. I have no idea what it might be. But it will come. This fight...it's gone on and on. But I have every intention on prevailing. And I will. No...Not this day. But someday, I'm positive. Yes, today I will regret, hurt and fear. But that's nothing new. I've plowed through this packed earth times before...and I'll do it again. I'm not giving up! It's got to get better. I just know. I'll defeat this enemy. Hold on...I'm not even gonna give it the status of being an "enemy". It's not worth it. Oh...but I must say...right now it's "holding all the cards". But going with that analogy...I Am the dealer. And going even further...I've been dealing bad hands! So, I do have a certain amount of direct responsibility to the prior failures. Wait a minute. I'm not gonna get into beating myself up...again. I've already put myself through enough pain. So, for now I'm gonna let go and just "blow it off". Man...If it were that simple. Anybody want to live in this mind?!!!

"The Find"

Clueless at the beginning. And for that
matter, the void of conclusion is a
mainstay through the entire past...and
up to the present. So do you let the
chains that bind just be...and not try to
find the key? No way!

Oh...there has been suffering with regards
to the issue. Sometimes conscious. Other
times subconscious. Such trickery. A game.
Is that it? Is it a puzzle that you have to solve?
And all a part of your life...your being.
How unfair it seems. You ask... "What's it
all about?" "What does it mean?" "Who is
this so-called person?"

You've been forthright and honest. You've
"laid all the cards on the table". "Your hand"...
you've let others see. There have been no
secrets...within just reason. But that answer...
it's still out in space. Looking for a connection
with your person. Such an endless search.

So many questions answered. So many doors
opened. So much earth plowed. And yet
more remains? Is such searching relevant to
security? In this matter...yes. Is it of the
spiritual? Well, in a "round about" way. But
its cause and effect are entangled with other
aspects of life. But the "God-thing"...it must
be addressed. And that brings some fright.

There is guidance. You are not by yourself.
Be grateful. Yes, I know you are thankful.
Is such "find" gonna make a spectacle? No.
It's personal. And will so remain. Only in
the abstract will it be revealed. Yet, there
are one or two confidants. For you know
you cannot "go it alone". A fact.

You're "honing-in" on the forever elusive
reason. Time will bring revelation.
Could be soon. Or to contradict, it may be
far in the future. But you have to try. You
must take action. By blind faith, you keep
"chipping away". Yes, it is a huge boulder.
The use of dynamite would wreck the soul.
Therefore, not an option.

In the meantime...during the quest...
how do you "hold yourself"? You must
draw strength...and you know where to
find such sustaining aid. It is above...
to your great fortune...it also lies within.
A spirit. Indeed, a spirit will appear.
Let it lead. Let go of useless weight.

Are you the only one who is on a path
of "seeking"? If most are truthful...No.
Recognitions, deductions, analysis...
all part of solving the mystery. Granted,
your goal is probably different than others.
In fact, all "destinations" are custom-made.

So, another day. Another attempt. "Wishful
thinking" does not hurt. It can serve as a
crutch necessary to "get by". Continue the
search. The light will shine. True account
will come to the forefront. And there will be
pain along the way...in all probability. When
"The Find" is unveiled, all the more rejoicing.

To Fly...To Soar

We get older and older. Perhaps there is a peak we reach, then stagnation or a decline follows. But for the fortunate this is not true. Fortunate? Sounds like a reference to "luck". NOT! No, if we always strive to be the best person using our positive God-given ability, we never fall short. Even when we are our own harshest critic. So it's up to us? Yes. Say, throughout life we have already grown and grown. We have reached heights we didn't think possible...with regards to our personal contentment and sanity. Actually, we have risen from a pit of despair. Should we be satisfied and rest? Maybe for periods of time. But if we want to keep what we have, we must set goals for the future. Perhaps we have to continue to set goals in order to survive. For the sake of a life worth living, we must make forward motion. Let's clarify...the forward motion must be beneficial to our person and an asset to society. Accomplishments... how gratifying, indeed. But the calendar turns, and there is more life to live. We have learned much in our lifetime. But there's still more insight to be digested and put into practice. No, it never stops. Damn. I want a vacation from emotional and mental delving which is necessary for making the next move. No? Well, ok...a mini-vacation is granted. Talking about that "delving", must it hold pain and fright? Usually. But the rewards of such action can sometimes change our "lot in life"... for the better. That sounds good. Yes, that's appealing and immensely desirable. So, we try harder when we feel "beat". A lot of the time there will not be immediate gratification even when we "bust our butt". So what? Such is the typical life. The "key" to growth...don't lower our standards. No matter how much we feel the urge to "give in". In fact, with each goal met, raise our standard. We've all heard..."The sky's the limit!" As for me, I'm "banking on it". The "everyday bird" flies. But the Eagle Soars!

The Tomcat

He's big and in the winter he's even bigger.
He curls up on the side of the house of which the sun
is the brightest. On a cold, cold night it seems he's
inside somewhere...an old shed or an unsuspecting
garage.

He's tough...scraps and rats. He also eats what the pet
cats eat, because it's their food. Yet he is not greedy.
Battle scars show, especially on his ears.
His head is as big as a pumpkin. And his hair is
matted.

The resident cats eventually accept him. Although,
social barriers are maintained and respected. He
becomes a part of the neighborhood, after our scares
and attempts to chase him off fail. Petting is foreign to
his breed.

There is a little sting inside...when we realize...several
weeks later...he won't be coming back.

SJB November 21, 1993

I Do What I Don't Want

Why? Why in the hell do I
do this to myself? Do I like
eventual grief? Can't I see
beyond the present?

Why lie to myself? Am I
really enjoying myself? I claim
that to be so...but. Keep it up.
Make myself miserable...again.

Give in? No, I won't. Gonna
do it my way. Oh...so that's
my reasoning? It makes so
much sense. Not!

Am I out of control? Yes.
Am I out of my control? No.
So, I have a choice in my actions?
Yes. And I choose to neglect
wisdom? It seems.

There's a slight desire. Yes, a
slight desire to do what is
reasonable. That's some comfort.
Maybe there's hope after all.

But I'm not there yet. It's been a
long time coming. And the light
I see is very dim. But there is a beam.
I must keep reaching for the positive.

Must I drive myself to madness before
I change? No. It will occur. There
will be release. Maybe not right now.
But I must go on the assumption that
the process will take place.

So, at this point...I do what I don't
want to do. Crazy...the whole thing.
Suffering is bound to be. It's a given.
A result of my being obstinate.

Let's back up to the slight positive.
I have to have something good to
feel about. Yes, it will be...I will
take a different path. But when?

So, I do what I don't want to do?
Be easy. Be kind. Breathe deep.
Let go of guilt and disgust.
Know prayers will be answered.
It's just gonna take more time.

In The Meantime

Waiting for the good. Not stagnant.
But no other avenue is in view at
this point. You're careful not to
look back. In the meantime, you
can't quiet see the next step. For if
you could, you'd most certainly move
forward.

A glance at the past will only bring
upset and anxious mind. Truly want
to avoid such path, which has already
been trod so often. In fact, that path
was your experience of life. And it
was miserable. Oh...someday, when
security prevails, a peek at bygone
destruction can aid in keeping on
course. But now is not the time.

The future. There seems to be a "feel"
of promise where concerned. Indeed…
a "freedom" appears to be the essence
of the "light at the end of the tunnel".
There is a "tug of war" inside. At times
a calm safety. Accompanied by high…
yet realistic expectations. And then
the opposite...such doubt, worry and
fear. You feel like a marked target of
your enemy...yourself.

So, avoiding what "has been"...while
focusing on the small opened window.
The window of successful, satisfying
assurance. And "the wait"...what can
be said? It's inevitable. But supposedly...
character and strength are built in the
longing.

Hold on. What are we saying here?
Well, endurance is being established
by having to be "ok" with "the now".
So...no, no answer yet. Also, it is
very possible a "trust" in self and
one's God is being honed. Wow!
What an acquisition! And it's basically
a result of "not having", in an immediate
fashion.

Well, here you sit. An unfinished product...
by far. What are you going to do? Make
the suffering more intense? No way! How
stupid! So, you must take your mind off
of "what's not". How? Maybe make
the "deal" not so "big". Yes...minimize the
effect. That is, what affect you have within
your control. So, you do have some "say-so"
after-all! Even if it's a small encouraging relief.

Ok. That's it. That's all that can be done...
right now. Be content in the knowledge that
things will eventually change for the better.
Lay low. "Fly under the radar" of lofty goals.
Not saying to lower your standards. Not at all.
But just "let go". Let it be. Continue to strive
to accomplish within the present realm. Above
all...be kind to yourself. Ease up. I believe the
day will come...the day of "release". In the
meantime, speak to yourself in the tone of a
warm, reassuring mother. Yes, in the meantime.

Just A Little More

Having risen a significant amount…
there is still upward motion necessary.
The bottom, it can be bad. But the
cellar never as extreme as before
the beginning of the climb. No…
God help me…never that hell again.

Four distinguishing threads of character.
Throw in abuse of substance, and no clarity
of personal identity…hmmm…What was
God thinking?

Three of the four…there's a "handle on".
But one more to fight, restrain, defeat.
Is it possible? Once a burning flame…
the inner workings have been reduced to
a flicker. Strength needed for combat.

There's a walk to walk. And hopefully
leading to a steady run. Where to begin?
Not sure yet. "Mind vacancy" where this
matter is concerned. Strategy needed
for further surge.

Yes, a plan. A plan for conquering is
absolutely necessary. What will it be?
It is not known...yet. But one is not
afraid to ask for help. The "asking"
is the only way the other characteristics
have been bridled. And it is ongoing.

So, today let's "layout" a design.
Guidance please. This one does not
know the way. There's weariness
from battling the other wars. But
now is not the time to give up.

Just a little more. More effort.
More time. More sacrifice. More
pain. More unravelling. More
delving. More, more, more...ugh!
How long to expect the "process"
to take? The tire is so evident.

Just a "little" more. But in the end, it
will be "big". Big change. Big comfort.
Big answers. Big success. Big joy.
Big, big, big...Yay! What will be
the catalyst? Have to believe...
It will be worth the work and the wait.

Fear Creeps

It's a kind of sick stomach.
But it's not a stomach ache.
Your mind tells you to make
a move. But you stand still.

It shouldn't be frightful.
There are no monsters or devils.
The lights are on. Darkness
doesn't have to be. And by choice…
the night has no clue.

The doors are locked. You know
your body is secure. Although…
once in a while you wonder. No…
Not apprehension from an intruder.
But flights of the mind. Where to
go for refuge?

Fear creeps silently. An aura
about the being. Fear seeps
slowly into close quarters. It
fills all empty spaces. Like liquid
permeating cracks and crevices.

So, where to hide if the substance
is within? Answer...nowhere.
Must face the culprit who is robbing
you of safety. It's a sense you can't
help but feel. Reason? Who knows?

Oh...it does not overwhelm.
Instead, it merely causes a scare that
nags and disrupts. Minor fear...yes.
That's the best description. Can it
be avoided? Yes and no.

How to defeat this culprit? Hmmm.
Perspective...Is it "that" big? Well, no.
But the discomfort of slight fright...
a sort of blind annoyance. Wait.
To say it annoys makes it seem a bit
too easy. And easy...it's not.

But back to fight. So, it is not enormous.
Good. But a type of poisonous thorn
piercing the skin. How to remove?
Gloves, protection from the "venom".
If not handled with care, it can course
through the veins.

What do we have? Perception...
it's basically a minute object. Ok.
Safeguard is needed. Have to use
ingenuity for that one. May take
awhile. Therefore...time. Ugh!

Alright God. It's going to be your
timetable. But hurry! I want this
to be over. What? Step back?
Let you be the lead? Let you play
the game? A game of which I've
previously lost...time and again.

This fear that creeps. You say it
really holds no power? Only that
which I give to its cause. Now...
now it's time for me to see its pitiful
potency. Reality...a funny thing.

Yes. One day the anxiety will be
wiped away. What is felt will no
longer hold serve. Release from
the snare...it will surely happen.
Till then...find something to hang
onto. Even if it's only brief in nature.

Triumph? It will soon astound.
Gates will be opened. Paths
will be cleared. The mind...
once a wretched enemy, it will
humbly retreat. Housing clear,
quiet and kind thought for self.

God's Will?

Sometimes we are certain to the deepest part of our being. Other times we are grasping at straws. Then again, we could be consciously or subconsciously avoiding and rejecting. What is it of which I speak? God's Will. Ugh! We are gonna have to take a look at ourselves. And sometimes the sight isn't very pretty. So, how do we know God's will for our life? Beats me! No...I'm over reacting to a subject that I at times, choose to deny. There are matters which are quiet obvious and should be heeded with little question. I believe those instances are usually associated with how we treat our fellow-man. And for me and my belief system... there are absolute spiritual laws that guide. They form my relationship with my Creator. So, there lies certainty. Many times I'm so sure that it's with ease that I follow direction. What about the "straw thing"? Man...What's up...what's down? Is it the truth or is it a false perception? Honestly, at times I have no idea. Are we "less than" if we find ourselves in such a position? I don't think so. We aren't made to know everything. But for me, I know I need to inquire as what to do. What's that called? Prayer. Oh...how little time I have to converse. What a human I am!! Get over it! Do the "right" thing. I might not know the right thing to do. But I do know it's the right thing to pray about the matter. Submission...that word kinda hurts my ears. Or should I say it drives a stake into my unbridled pride. So, I either choose what has been revealed to my heart, or pretend that I don't know the answer and insist to keep on looking. What a joke! Then there's the "big one"...I just don't want to do what I know is right. I don't want to do God's will. Watch out! There are traps for sure. All the while, I know it's going to "catch up with me". And yet...well, I fall short of God's standards. Thing is, He doesn't make the standards impossible for me to attain. No, with His help they're within my reach. But I just "flat- out" refuse to follow His lead. Well, what more can I say about that? This... There are consequences. I'll surely pay the price. Nothing more. So, how can I "wrap-up" this writing to serve a purpose? I mean I've stated what I believe to be facts. That's it...yes, I've answered my question to finding God's will. Free will. Again, my gracious and caring God leaves the decisions up to me. It could be called a type of "freedom of religion". In essence... to choose. To choose what I'm lead to believe is God's will for my life. And it all goes back to what? To prayer. Taking time to "check-in" with my Maker. Asking to be shown the way. Then carrying out His plan to the best of my honest understanding. So easy. So hard. So just!

By Design

I'm different. My looks.
My tone of voice. My
actions and reactions.
My moods. My feelings.
My thoughts. My beliefs.

I like sports. I like rock music.
I like old people. I like to write.
I like cats and dogs. I like
walking about college campuses.
I like fishing. I like talking.

I am a female. I am a daughter.
I am a sister. I am an aunt.
I am a great-aunt. I am a
Christian. I am a native Texan.
I am an Arkansan.

I have been to college. I have
eaten oxtail. I have spent nights in
a fraternity house at Oregon State...
(Just to clarify for my reputation...
it was summer break...almost vacant.)
I have danced at a "dive" on Proctor
Street - Port Arthur, Texas. (Not gonna
try to salvage reputation on that one!)

I worked as a recreation trainer.
I worked in a cereal chemistry laboratory.
I worked as an advertisement paper
sales representative. I worked at
many odd...some Very Odd jobs.

I am kind. I am fair. I am nice.
I am hard-headed. I am thoughtful.
I am disturbed. I am reliable.
I am short-tempered. I am honest.
I am cautious and I am foolish.

I can show compassion. I can
guide others, looking for direction.
I can apply what I've learned.
I can "make a mess" of situations.
I can open doors...literally and figuratively.
I can fillet fish...well, ok. I can make roux.

I want to see Mt. Rushmore. I want to
publish a book. I want to overcome
weaknesses. I want to beat disorders.
I want to go to the College Baseball
World Series in Omaha, Nebraska.

I was born. I live. I will die.
I was created by design...by a
Creator who deserves my heart and
immense praise. I am special.
I "broke the mold".

You are a human. You are my neighbor.
You are my responsibility where witness
of the Almighty is concerned. You are
unique. You are special. You are to be
respected. You are my friend. Most
of all...You are loved by God. Claim that
love...it's yours...by design.

The Dark Undercurrent

It began at first breath.
It remains to this day.
Sometimes it blatantly glares.
Other times it barely glimmers.

This life continues to be peeled.
An uncovering to the core.
Will it ever end? These unpleasant
features of the being. A glimpse
of the center is beginning to be seen.
Scary. God have mercy!

Other troubles...many overcome.
Hard work on the constant wage
of war has brought victories so
precious. Guides on the left and
right shed light and show the way.

But knowledge alone is not enough.
Steps must be taken. Discouragement
sways...but there must not be surrender.
Yes, there are more battles to be won.
Put on more armor. The mind must
be protected by any means possible.

The dark undercurrent. It possesses
an evil aspect. Is it a spiritual flaw?
No. But there is belief that aid from
heaven can come with prayer. So,
falling to one's knees is common.

This talk. Does such gut wrenching
truly exist? Or is it just a "conjuring up"
of weak humanity? Is an understanding
ever possible? Maybe not. And if
that should be the case...acceptance a
must. To accept is not defeat.

Oh...how we are designed. Doesn't
make sense...to us. Why this allotment
of agony? Is perseverance the goal of
our time on earth? Who knows? It
seems unfair. Are we automatically
due justice in life? Why not? That is
the perception.

So, it is what it is. What to do?
Fight...and continue to fight regardless
of negative outcomes. We are born
with breathing a natural inclination, even
when questioned. So, more the stride.

The dark undercurrent. So baffling.
So consuming. Dissection to break
the force is desired. Is it attainable?
Perhaps. Regardless, there must be
effort. Let the bodily senses supply
support...even if frayed.

The dark undercurrent. So deep.
So black. To call it "eerie" gives
no respect to its power. The
devastation reeked not to be surpassed
by simplistic glad tidings. No. Supreme
might is necessary.

So, scream out for help! Grab hold
of any object of secure substance.
Follow advice which seems plausible.
Rely on others. Do not hide. Do not
remain alone. Speak the words of
strife. Let it be known. Trust, if
possible.

Faith and hope. Both have to exist.
The need for their properties absolute.
But how? So tired, weary and worn.
Yes, it has been long. Rest. Then
stand once more. Believe there
is a reason...even if not seen.

"In my Father's house are many mansions."
"Give us this day our daily bread."
"Get up and walk."
"When you do this for the least of these."
"Be still and know that I am God."

One hour the dark undercurrent will be
no more. It will be banished...no longer
to exist. Peace...yes peace will replace
despair. It may be soon...or far-off.
But praise! It will be endless. I say
forever and ever! How great that day!

And Another Thing...

When do we talk? When do we shut up?
Oh...such bold and abrasive questions.
My ears, they hurt. Am I to only listen?
Why do you have the privilege of voice?
And for me...silence is required?

When do we talk? When we truly have
something of value to convey. When we
want to express our feelings. When we
want to entertain. When we want to get
our point across. When we sympathize.
When we "lift up" spirits on earth and on high.
When we address hurt, pain and discord.

When do we shut up? When we whine.
When we complain. When we hurt another.
When we lie. When our voice is inappropriately
loud. When our tone rings of hate. When
substance of matter is absent. When we argue.
When we boast to the extreme. When all
said is of the negative. When we mislead.

So, let our voice resemble pleasing song.
Know if someone admonishes our spoken
word...it could be to our benefit. And more
than likely...also theirs. Respond to...rather
than push forth.

The time is hard. Hurt abounds. This is when the touch means so much more than verbal enabling. A smile...yes facial expression tells it all. We keep our "knowledge" to ourselves... such as it is. And with mouth closed, we can listen and hear. Yes, someone else is in the room. Respect.

What will happen? There will be development. Of what? Peace, happiness, love, appreciation. Don't we so desire such? Of course! And that precious silence...absence of talk is not always avoidance. Rather it is just letting one another be. Be what? Be themselves. Shut up and let others show. Show what? Concern, support, consistency and gratitude.

So, there is a time to speak. And there is a time to simply be quiet. With practice, we'll learn the ropes. Learn how to be tactful in expressing our viewpoints. Learn how to say "I love you."... and truly mean it. Learn with silence, we can gain even more knowledge. Hear others express charity towards our lives. Then there will be security in our emotions. Enough said.

The Deeper We Dig

The deeper we dig...what's to be found? Is it only memories and reminders of regrets and mistakes? Re-enforcing our undesirable frailty? A source of disgust within ourselves? Well, it doesn't have to be all negative. No, not at all. What happens when we dig? Yes, there may be delicate and somewhat uncomfortable finds. But on the other hand, we may see the beginning of a new existence. And the newness we "come upon" inside, may possess an extremely positive thread. How great that can be! Just think...a chance to "start over". Wait a minute, are humans afforded such an opportunity? I mean...realistically. I can only speak for myself. And I've found with some introspection...yes, a new path is there to be trod. The "fresh start"...perhaps it holds a future full of hope and endless grand experiences. Can I hope for such? Should I hope for such? The digging... there's the fear of falling into feelings that are less pleasing. Maybe much fright ahead. As for me, I have recently "opened a door" leading to a hallway that is bright and promising. Has it taken hard work? Yes. And strong efforts must always continue. But "easier times", they begin to be evident. All so worthwhile. A chance for a sane, happy and very content life starts to surface. Oh...I've already been blessed in many ways. But now MORE!! Yes, more "gifts to unwrap". And all these exceptionally good vibes...they are truly flowing through the body's veins? Yes. Heart, mind and soul. Sounding "near perfection"? By no means.

There will always be trials and tough times. But back to what has evolved with "the dig"...sanity, happiness and contentment. More than previously experienced. Will the night be oh so "black"? At times. Will the sun rise and the way be shown? Yes, indeed. I just have to continue to dig deep and discover what's meant to be. Along the way, don't be too proud to accept comfort, consolation and guidance from my brother. And forever be grateful.

Nearing Change

It will not come as a shock.
The path to the desired destination
has been arduous...to say the least.
But what happens when you work
hard? Usually, great benefits!

So the continuous catharsis...has it
been in vain? I'm beginning to
think not. A sense. Yes, only a
sense is being noted. And a belief
that more is to come.

This "feeling", it mixes with the
complicated, intense and at times
very cruel mind. So, what exactly
is taking place? I'm not sure. But
it is good. It has a "lightness". And
a dim beam at the end of the long dark
corridor is starting to appear.

A "letting go". A release of conflict.
Could it be? A change is nearing?
I believe so. Is my prediction too
hasty? I don't think. For there is a
"way" that cannot be denied. Clarity
of the thought processes in the possible
future. Oh God...let it be reality.

Will I try to make it be? No. It must
just "take place". A push or shove
would only be a detriment to the
possible evolvement. It has been slow
in coming. Grueling tasks and heavy toil
have been the prescription.

Yes. I believe the peace which has
been so elusive, may be on the horizon.
Oh, peace with other concerns has been
present for a long time. No doubt. Yet...
an absence of one nature, now so blatantly
obvious. And with this observation comes
the ability to solve. Pieces to the puzzle.

A life road so easily walked? Unheard of.
As many can attest. And this one, being a
type of survivor. It could have been much
harder. Praise God...not! So many at a
loss for hope. Lord, have mercy on them.

Help. It has come from others and within.
Due to a King and many loyal subjects...
there has been promise. Yes, security
even when not felt. No...At times little
credence should be given to thought and
feelings. A dismissal towards a natural
inclination. Scary, but necessary.

A friend talked of "freedom". And that is the goal...the objective...the desire. Chains breaking. That's what is perceived at this moment. And may it continue. Not to ever end. For now, simply a sense. That will suffice to produce further effort.

This write will now end. But clearly a "start" has taken place. What will happen tomorrow? Only the Ultimate Authority can know. Continue to work. Continue to be. Continue to rest. At ease. Yes... a calm must be nurtured. Allow guidance. And let a healthy love of self, begin to flourish. Nice.

And All The People Said "Amen"!

Attendance was counted.
There were more than usual.
Everybody said "Amen".
But did it really matter...the number?

The choir was elegantly robed.
Their voices blended pleasantly.
Everybody said "Amen".
But was perfection necessary for their performance?

The plates were passed.
Paper and coins began to fill.
Everybody said "Amen".
Did material wealth make the congregation?

The preacher spoke words with authority.
People listened and learned.
Everybody said "Amen".
Did it make a difference if the child in the pew slept?

The hymn of invitation was sung.
Some spirits were moved.
Everybody said "Amen".
The ones who came forth...were they the only people touched?

The doors opened and those in attendance began to leave.

Most felt joy, relief, fulfillment, purpose.

Everybody said "Amen".

Does it matter what they do, where they go, what they say?

Absolutely.

The Behavior

Oh...how cruel the behavior.
It goes on and on. When will
the end be in sight? And it is
all self-inflicted. Ridiculous...
in others' sight.

A miserable state has become
the usual. The answer seems so
practical. Yet...it is "out there".
Far from reach.

The tired, dull pain wants to shed
tears. But they do not come. An
unfortunate characteristic...at times.
For some release would bring relief.

Can't it be controlled? Why can't
more effort be applied? It would
indeed be the "cure"...so others think.
But what about the pained? Continual
attempts may not be seen by some.
But the one hurting knows different.

So, this acutely negative behavior...
Will scolding or threats be a solution?
It has not worked thus far. No, in
fact harsh words only bring resentment.
Definitely no resolve.

For the moment, the behavior thrives.
And the one affected bears the burden.
But just for the while. There will be
a salvation. One is determined to
remain steadfast. Peace will come.

There is much hope that a new
approach will bring rest and recuperation.
Yes, the madness will stop. One just
has to "hold tight". Time. It will take
more time. And the involved has all
the time in the world...unfortunately.
Because their time is a detriment to the
cause. It only produces confusion.

But wait...back to the positive. There
will be cessation of the trial. One has
faith in the help to come. Beauty will
once again reign. The behavior will
be crushed...one is certain. "Soon!"...
One silently screams. And the plea
will be heard.

Do We Ever "Get There"?

Tell me. Do you EVER "get to the
bottom of things"? Well...I guess
since life is an ongoing process until
death...the answer would be "no".
Damn. Finality, a type of closure,
"the end"...leaving a new start. Such
attainment is so hoped. But...well,
that's not always reality.

You've dug deep into your being...
mind, heart and soul. And what is the
outcome? Still a lack of clarity. Did
you not try hard enough? No, you
gave it your all. And many results
have brought about astonishing change...
for the better. But there is more?!!

Yes. More work is necessary for further
evolvement into the person you wish to
become. Confrontations may take place.
Not to belittle. But to "breakdown" false
beliefs and concepts. This is not comfortable
for anyone...the one invoking or the person
who seems to be but a victim. Growth
usually "calls" for this procedure.

How to approach this endless search to seize?
Calmly, carefully, collectively, considerations.
Beat the fear of the unknown. Not the scare
death brings...but an honest look within. What
will be found? Do you really want to know?
To remain in purgatory...no. A desire to rise
to completion. Not that it's gonna come...but
it's in the trying that the actions fulfill the
needed want.

So, more toil is the "prescription". Oh, so
tired. Well, rest a bit. Maybe a different
perspective will take over. Easing the
difficulty involved to "get to the bottom
of things". Follow methods advised by
the respected, and the answers will come.
But be ready...there'll be another "bottom"
to your life with which you must deal.

No. Don't go blaming God...nor others.
It just is. It's life. And perhaps view it
in this manner. The more "bottom of
things"...the more gained along the way.
Possibly, very delightful aspects which
bring a positive wonderment. Appealing?

"Fundamentalism"

The exclusion of so many.
For the security of a few.
All in the name of God.

SJB October 26, 1992

Two Miraculous Evolutions of Living

1. Pains of the past can lessen with time.
2. Past pleasures have the ability to take a path of
   enduring fondness.

SJB November 4, 1993

Don't Take It Personal!

To not include me in your world is personal.
To propose I'm not included in God's world...
is attempting to speak for one of God's Three Persons.

SJB December 25, 1993

And Yet, More Work

It is true. It will never be complete
until last breath is drawn. But come
on...more settling necessary? The
best possible is desired. Looking
for a world with more satisfaction
and security.

Present from the beginning...
the darkness, stumbling blocks, pains.
At times thought to be conquered.
And yes, at times they were beat.
But these ferocious animals, they
can come back to life.

Has it been a lie...the positive results
of hard work? No. Much good has
occurred. In fact, many miracles.
But maybe now the beasts reveal
themselves in minute fashion. Just
enough to cause discomfort.

The skin is not as tough as previously...
past times when reprieve was never
a part of living. Yes, without having
to battle so fiercely...strength and
muscle tone has decreased. Actually,
discomfort is too "light" of a word to
describe. Turmoil exists too easily.

So, a new attack is planned. Some of
the weapons are different than the past.
In fact, some are rather strange and
unusual. But it's definitely worth the try.
For more happiness and contentment is
sought. Much hope is present. Grateful.

Will it happen too soon? Unfortunately, no.
Time. More time and much effort. Like
before...struggles, fears, disappointments
will be reality. But in the end, the results
will be worth the fight.

So, the process shall start. Believe God
will give endurance during the while.
How to begin? Like always, an inner
view. Privately, dissection and purging
will take place. The first course...
a pen and legal pad. Guidance from a
qualified confidant. No, not alone.
Thankful.

Guitars

Everybody likes guitars. Don't they? Why, of course. All kinds of music are played. I prefer when they "blare out" "rock". But wait...I also love James Taylor's expression of art and talent. So much "out there" to enjoy. I had several of the particular instrument. My first guitar was solid wood. About four feet in length, it was rather slender. It could also make a ball sail through the air. No strings. Just tape wrapped around the grip. A baseball bat. I played the "oldies" on that guitar. You know...the late 60's. There was an evolution of the guitar in my life, for my next did have strings! I could strum...but no sound. What was it? A badminton racket. I distinctly remember standing on top of my twin bed, kinda bouncing...playing and singing the Baptist hymn "At Calvary". My sister "caught me". Due to her laughter...a "make-fun-of" laughter...I decided to perform in private, thereon out. Next came "the real deal"...well sorta. My Dad, brother and I were in Gibson's Discount Store. I saw it! A red, plastic electric guitar...with an amplifier!! WOW!!! Since, my older brother and sister had spoiled Santa Claus for me, I pleaded with my Dad. And how about that...the "real" Santa came through! This guitar had nylon strings, and of course it came with a couple of picks. So, I was set. But somehow the amplifier didn't "spill out" tunes that sounded kin to our family stereo. Disappointed, I began using that instrument as a World War II rifle. Have I mentioned I had quiet an imagination as a youngster?!

Several years passed, and I was nearing junior high. Our family made one of our trips to Arkansas to see grandparents, aunts, uncles and cousins. Well, I was in luck. My older cousin had bought an actual acoustic guitar...I think by saving Green Stamps. He...being one of five boys, the instrument broke soon after the purchase. I showed interest in the musical device even though it was "disassembled". Because of prodding by my grandmother, my cousin said I could have the broken guitar. Actually, his brother really wanted it, but I "won out". I felt kinda bad...well, kinda. So, back in Beaumont, my Dad used much glue to make it "like new". I can't remember how the strings were put in order...but they were in correct accord. I taught myself the chords...G-7, C, and D-7...I think that's right. I'm not really musically knowledgeable. I bought a beginners' book. Learned a few of old time folk-like songs. Strumming chords only...of course. I was pleased with myself. I even wrote two songs for a "play" that my cousin, neighbor and myself "put-on" for our parents. They never made the Top 40! Alas, my fingers hurt when I tried to play. The once broken guitar kept getting "out of tune". Then the wood started cracking. Soon, I gave up. Oh...every once in awhile I'd pick it up and try to "make do" and express my inner soul. Not for anyone to hear...most definitely! Years and years passed. All I did during that time was play the "air guitar". Usually, after consuming libations! I'm sure I made a unique impression. Then came the late 1990's. An adult...an adult who experienced manic episodes. So, it was then that I began to pursue becoming a rock star! That's right. What thu hell?!! I didn't know "jack-shit". I decided it would be good to become the bass player of a band. But I thought...first I need to "get" the basics of an acoustic. So, not having ample resources...I went to a reputable music store in Beaumont...used money I needed for necessities...and bought a brand name guitar. I was cool!! I was "on my way"! I bought a couple of books that had rock songs made simplified. I didn't want to just learn chords, I wanted to really play. Needless to say, I attained neither goal. But I tried hard...at times. Those times that my attention span allowed. Well, at one point I felt I had learned "Hotel California" good enough for some friends to hear. I struggled, and somehow in my distorted mind I thought my performance deserved applause. My friends were holding a conversation during my concert. When I finished, I waited for a response. None coming...I said "What do you think?" My friend then said "What was that?" Hell, I never really liked him anyway!! I was somewhat discouraged, yet in my mind I still thought an electric bass was an option... leading to stardom. Fortunately, it wasn't long before the psychiatric episode began to decline. So, about guitars...don't you love'em?! I do. But I have decided to strive for other accomplishments. I mean...guitar players are "a dime a dozen"!

You Know Me?

So, you think you know me. You say you've "got my number". Careful. Your knowledge of me might be rather limited, if the truth be known. And I can say the same for my ability to be certain of what "makes your boat float". Am I saying we are all strangers? No. But I believe no matter how much we "give out", there always lies within each of us at least a speck of "mystery". A part of our being that our own self might only catch a glimpse...on a good day. For instance, take me. I write, talk, expose much more than most people. But everything? Well, I've stated many times..."I've left no stone unturned." But I must say that is in regards to issues which must be tended to and resolved. So, what about this "mystery"? What's with that? I think it is an emotion which cannot be handled by anyone except myself and my Maker. No, not even the best psychotherapist. And I hold several counselors who know me in extreme high regard. But they have their limits. For they can only guide me. They can only take me to the entrance of my "insides". From there I step into the "mystery" alone. Save my Maker. Thank God. Oh, these helpers...they suggest, they hold, they comfort. But when the "lights go out"...it's just me and my Maker. Note how many times I've included "my Maker"? It's for real, people. We have to live by ourselves. Yes, there can be another human oh so close. And yet, in our being...a "piece", however small it may be...it rests in our souls, invisible to all. And you know what? We have to live with it. Is it scary? Sometimes. Is it a source of security? Sometimes. However it "lays claim"...the bottom line...we have to "turn it over" to our Maker. Whew!! That's a relief. Our depths...they can be "entrusted" to a Supreme Being. We are "let off the hook" with regards in our ability to make sense of the "mystery". So, what of all this talk? What is really being said? Well, we come into this world surrounded by bright lights and held by loving arms. But when we leave...on our way out...it's a step we take all by our earthly selves. The Good News...when breathing that last breath, our lungs are filled with fresh air. Oxygen which is the life source for the dimension we are about to enter. Back to the "mystery"...the part of our inner self with which we may or may not have come to terms. My belief...the question will be answered, the void filled, the puzzle solved. And there will be a "peace" which envelopes and surpasses my highest expectations in an unfathomable manner. Oh Happy Day!

Fleeting Thought and No Thoughts

You remember that commercial concerning drug abuse: "The mind is a terrible thing to waste."? Well, my saying: "The mind is a terrible thing...period!" Each individuals' thought processes are so amazing and unique. Often I say..."You don't EVEN want to take a look inside my head!" It can be rather scary. I say that with truth and humor. I look back at my first hospitalization, not knowing just how severe my Obsessive-Compulsive Disorder was at the time. What did I know? It was how I always thought...since birth. For the first month that I was in the hospital, it seemed an endless searching for why I was there...besides being depressed. Or was it really depression? Others seemed to have reasons for their despair. I had not been through a life of horrible experiences of which I heard. So, there was an element of guilt...like I was just taking up space that someone else really needed. And of course, I had a certain amount of resistance to suggestions made and options offered...they didn't apply to me. Again, what did I know? There was safety in the way things had always been. A false perception. But somehow what the hospital program was teaching me was apparently starting to have some impact. All along, my mind would assume things. Such as...why the doctor looked at my chart an "unusual" length of time, why the music therapist played a certain song, why I was the third person instead of the fourth to receive their medications...you get my gist. At any rate, about a month and a half into the program the first "breakthrough" occurred. It was morning. I'd just woke up and went to wash my face. As I lifted my head from the sink, looking into the glass-like piece of tin, a thought shot through my mind..."Maybe the nurses aren't against me." The thought was fleeting and didn't last, but it was the beginning to a change of my thought processing. I was letting my defenses down... allowing a different train of thought to occur which had never happened before in my life. It was very strange to say the least. In retrospect, throughout all my life, my mind had been racing constantly. And for the most part, a build-up of negative preoccupations. Well, this fleeting thought was to be just the beginning of a tearing down of chain reactions within. So, time passed. It was now about a month later. I had adjusted to the hospital program, interacted with others and participated willingly in all the therapeutic activities. I actually liked being there. And I was participating a great deal in group psychotherapy. Although, I somewhat continued to feel as if I didn't deserve to be there. The other patients had "real" problems. I was still trying to clarify that my vague sense of psychiatric problems were justifiable. A real loner amongst loners. But that perception was about to change its course... somewhat. I woke up one morning and went through the usual hospital routine prior to group therapy. When I went into the first session, I took a seat. There were about 12 patients in the room. Marjorie was the therapist. She was a tiny, kinda plain-jane woman. Probably in her early 60's. She shut the door, sat down and without even glancing at the others, looked directly at me and asked..."Sara, what's on your mind?" This surprised me that she approached me so immediately. I didn't really know what was going on. So in response to her question... "Sara, what's on your mind?" I kinda looked into space and replied..."Nothin'." Without any hesitation, she quickly raised both her arms in the air, and with a huge smile said..."YES!!" I was still sitting there kinda like an "airhead" wondering what was going on. But briefly it went through my mind...Oh, this is what they've been getting at...maybe? The rest of the day I was in somewhat of a different "space". I didn't know what to think because...well, because there weren't a load of thoughts in my head. My racing mind was not only being harnessed, but some of it was being disposed of. And this was just a "dent" in my thought processes. Much more freedom and release was to come through the years. Albeit slowly. To this day, it continues. Truly a miracle. So grateful and thankful.

New Spirit Evolving?

Could the time be coming? No...
Not a new reign on earth. Not
the cure to fatal illnesses. The
solution to hate and discord? Nope.
The end of divorce, crime, abuse
and addictions? Unfortunately, no.

So, what is it that one thinks may
be on the horizon? Well, it can
be found dwelling in the deepest
part of the being. Ok...is it good
or bad? It's Good! WHAT?!!!
Really? After such excess of
tangled and difficult emotions.

Tell about it. Well, much work
has been put forth for achievement.
How so? Basically, honest talk and
write. That's all?! So simple. No,
far from simplicity. A searching and
exposure with regards to facts and
feelings. Most already "dealt with".
But for some reason a "peace" was
not produced with the expulsion.

More about what's expected. Actually…
the change is presently in its infant stage.
A lesser encroachment on the mind by
a sinister viewpoint of self. Enormous
sigh of longed for relief is starting
to accompany breath. Wow! And
for some reason, there doesn't seem to
be the fear of possible jinx. Great!

With this beginning departure of
disrespect towards oneself…well,
what's taking its' place? A "lighter
sense" surrounding daily events.
And less complication this person
usually "brings to the table", with
regards to endless thinking. A
"hush" starting to "blanket".

Where will this newness lead?
Not sure. But it is believed a
more pleasant existence will be
one result. If that is to be all
the acquisition…that is indeed more
than ever expected in this lifetime.
And much gratitude will be due!

She Sang Soprano

It was the 70's...so her hair style showed.
The dress, she had sewn. Her jewelry was
a flower pin attached to the dress. But all
was covered with a robe. A garment she
claimed could get hot and stuffy.

It was Sunday...she was in the choir loft.
Surrounded by friends, she had a smile on
her face. She took her role very seriously.
She sang soprano.

She had a "birds'-eye" view. Therefore
my antics were limited. Once she looked
directly at me...seemingly to encourage me
to "step-out". After that I avoided her eyes.

A couple of times she sang "a special".
She didn't give herself enough credit for
her ability. And once or twice a duet.
She sang soprano.

There was always excitement over
the Christmas Cantata. Extra rehearsals
besides the usual Wednesday night practice.
Most of the time, she "caught" a ride home
with a fellow soprano...who lived the next
street over.

What a blessing. Every Sunday knowing
right where my mother was going to be.
Able to look up and see the one who provided
safety, security, meals, clean clothes, and
unconditional love. Not to mention the warm
lap in which many times I rested my head.

Now, she sings the same song over and over.
Much of the time she makes up her own verses.
She's not standing in a sanctuary while she sings.
She's sitting in a wheeled chair among those who
pay no attention. Unpleasant noises can drown
out her voice. She sings soprano, alto or whatever
comes out.

What a blessing. I still know where I can find
my mother every Sunday. Someday she will
no longer be in sight. She will be in heavens'
choir. Joining friends who went before her.
She'll be one more angel who's singing soprano!

About Security

Does security prevent physical harm?
No. But it says...you'll recover.

Is security a factor dealing wealth?
Only if you already possess the means.

Can security abolish doubt?
No. It says...trust me once more.

Does security assure no tears?
No. But it does dry them.

Is security limited to a certain sect?
Not so. It is abundant for all...just ask.

Can security control thinking?
No. But silently it eventually eases the mind.

Does security have a voice?
Not necessarily. And if not, other senses can convey.

Does security put food on the table?
Not without a certain amount of toil.

Can security prevent war?
No. But it can re-establish order.

Does security eliminate fear?
No. But it provides a safe haven.

Where can security be found?
It is based in faith. Even the faultiest of faith.

How can I obtain security?
"Knock...and the door shall be opened."

How can I keep security?
Let it dwell and grow by the Ultimate Power.
Then follow with Much Thanksgiving!

Humility

Humility. Not necessarily a bad word. Oh...it can bring anger, embarrassment, a feeling of "less than". But one can also grow from experiences which are uncomfortable. Tonight I was "humbled" publicly. In my support group, I was told to basically..."shut up". I was a bit mad at my mentor who had "called me down". So what did I do that was so bad? Nothing...I hadn't been "bad". I merely needed to be reminded that what I have to say doesn't always need to be heard. Long ago I would have been very mad and resentful. Maybe "taken her to task" within my mind or argue the point. But I didn't. Not to say it didn't bother me...I'm human. But I didn't want to crawl under the table and hide with shame. No, I simply and somewhat humorously said "Ok...I've said enough, I'll shut up. I get the message." Did I think about it much after the fact? Why, yes. Who wouldn't? Oh...I counted a few of what I tend to consider her "downfalls". Whether or not that "holds water", that is her business. So, what is good about being humbled? It lets you know you are not the "center of the universe". You realize that not all you believe in, applies to everyone. In my case, tonight it told me what I had to say held no relevance to the topic of which we were speaking. And in the end, when I dissected a bit of the occurrence...I realized that I had been guided in the "right direction". Not just in the instance at hand, but in life. I was made a better person. I can be "wrong" and it's "alright". No need to run, boil in my gut, hold resentments, or cover my face. Being humbled can make one stronger. And it is absolutely necessary for living among others and relating to God. So, yeah... kinda embarrassing. But so much gained! Thankful.

True Identity

Parents, birthdate, birthplace,
successes, failures, belief system,
desires, dreams...all these and
much more...already known.
But as sure of name...so uncertain
the "aspect" that prevents the
completion of absolute sanity.

So, it is not finished. The quest for
"reasons why". Is it a farce to think
that such knowledge should be
obtained? I mean, everything can't
be known. Of course, it is not a
given human privilege to understand
all. But a "feel" of wholeness is not
out of the question. In fact, one should
strive for such.

Do I really know me? Well, I believe I
know a lot about me. But is that the
same? Maybe. Maybe not. Is deep
introspect only a deterrent to contentment?
Perhaps on this particular day...it is.
Actually, it is ventured to suspect
the lack of complete recognition and
understanding of thought and action, leaves
inconsistency in perception of self.

Are you saying I don't know me from Adam?
No. In fact, no voice has yet spoken. It's all
in the mind. By damn...it's Always in the mind!
You're not involved in this process. It's up to
my being to investigate and consider vague
purpose. So much. So much...already identified.
And still...there is more? As I live and breathe...
yes, there will always be more.

But let's consider this...a part...a piece...not yet
reckoned. If complete fulfillment is to be
acquired, it must be "faced" and significant
work among its secrets necessary for honest
accomplishment. This action is a must in
order for absolute security. That is...security
within self.

The game plan. Hold on tightly to what is known.
Continue to claim what has already proven to be
true and faithful. Don't fret or seek flight. It would
only lead to helpless fear and anger. Of course,
fear and anger concerning what is unknown already
exist. But don't "add fuel to the fire".

Why dare examine what is probable to bring confusion, pain and uncomfortable intensity of emotion? Because. Because there has to be resolve in order to move forward. Also, there is the desire to know my true identity. Yea, yea...I know who I am. But then again... this speck in my person. This unrevealed portion. My "makeup"...it demands the mystery to be solved. And I will not settle for a life that is "less than". God guide me.

And They Tire...

It goes on. It continues.
There seems to be no end.
Why? Because "it is what it is".
Always striving for change.
But solution does not appear readily.

It gets old. The same thing.
Not a pleasant course.
Searching...always searching.
An answer will surely come.
You have faith this to be true...
when positive tones are present.

How long will it last?
This is not to be known.
Claims to possible resolve surface.
You see glimmers. There is a bit of hope.
And they tire.

Have you mislead them by false belief?
No. Honesty has always been a quality.
They want happy. But it cannot be produced.
As already stated...It gets old.
It lingers and lingers.
And they tire. You tire. It has been long.

Is there any fault? You take on guilt.
But nothing has been done wrong.
You perceive the negative. You assume.
Assumptions cannot be afforded.
Perhaps you are mistaken. Very possible.
Yes, they may tire. But they remain.

What to do? Endure, respect, "take" more action.
Things will change. It won't last forever...
regardless of the eternal charge within.
This thing...the mind...these thoughts...
so twisted into a view of doom.
They are tired. You are tired.

Once more...What to do?
Take note. Have you forgotten?
Dedication. Allegiance. Devotion.
These characteristics they have.
Of course they tire. But what's this?
They love. You love.
And love will supersede.

At Ease...For Real?!!!

It's so seldom. It's so elusive.
This body and mind relaxed.
No. Everyday situations have
not changed drastically. But
there is a reprieve. Yes, an
absence of continuous and
repetitive thought.

It's almost magical. Though, no
magician is present...at least not in
human form. There has been
stress...but taken in stride. Afraid
to ask the cause. Don't want to
delve. For fear of cessation.

Actually, lack of delving or digging
is one of the characteristics. How
nice. Yes, it's nice not to think and
think. All the questioning within...
not to be found. A gracious angel
has descended on the brainwaves.

Worry? Very little. And yet so many
confounded issues not resolved. Hmmm.
Fears abound, but at this moment they
have no power. What a wonder!
Is a falsehood the reason for this
"vacation"? Wait...it doesn't really
matter if that is the case.

Take it. Accept it. Rest for the weary.
Don't count the days. Don't watch
the clock. For sure it will end...
as with all good things. And that's
to be expected...just life.

Sing in response to the lack of
suffering. Don't take for granted
the "gift" that has been given.
Give adoration to the One who
has offered such emotional
clearance. And along with joyful
song...DANCE!!!

My...How They Pale

Problems and issues. So important, life changing and time consuming. Today, I struggled fiercely with my own personal psychological issues, and with the constant unavoidable caregiver frustrations. Stress and hopelessness took hold. As humans, it's impossible to "run from" these responsibilities, if we are honest in making the best of our life. In fact, that's why I refer to the issues as "responsibilities". If we deep down care on resolve, it is indeed up to us to see that an answer comes forth. Even though I felt downtrodden today, I attended a meeting tonight in which others discussed obstacles they were facing. But solution was available for the taking. Quick resolve was not promised...but in time, resolution was guaranteed. That is, if effort would be applied. As I listened to other people "spill-out" their problems, mine began to pale. Part of the reason was assuredly due to placing myself in a different environment. But most of the transforming of how I viewed my situation was because I "listened to" and gave input concerning those friends lives. How tangled and immense were their predicaments. They didn't have a clue how to fight their "demons". And I looked at myself. I have a plan of action, professionals guiding and confronting me, and supportive family and friends who listen. Given the whole experience tonight, I was able to put my problems into a different perspective that actually has a positive tone. No longer does what I have facing me "eat my lunch". I went away from the meeting somewhat refreshed. No, it was not that I had "made too much of things" earlier in the day. They are real and I must deal with the distressing facts. But I have a much needed reprieve from the upheaval in my mind. Tomorrow, I will try to continue to hold onto the realization that I can handle the issues with which I deal every day. Truly grateful for the people in my life and a God who can provide relief!

As We Cry

Tears are shed.
Sounds of wailing.
Gasping to verbalize.

Face reddens.
A scowl frightens those present.
Yells fill the vacant air.

Eyes droop.
Sorrow, a feeling, has a face.
Lips tighten with fear of breaking silence.

Hysteria.
So inappropriate for the cause.
Loud giggling embarrasses.

Flailing recklessly.
Extreme presentation of body movements.
Others depart the somewhat dangerous scene.

Listlessness.
A vacant appearance is still.
Dull sounds encompass words.

And we all feel pain.

Peace of The Puzzle

It's been a long road. Looking.
Searching. Seeking. Longing to
be in total accord with my Master.
Well, due to the human aspect...
it will never be "total" until the
next world.

One wants to make the Author
of their life happy and pleased.
He calls for complete reliance.
Desiring our fellowship...even
the least compatible.

How fortunate we are...He wants
us! Just as we are, we humble
ourselves and present ourselves.
And He readily accepts us.
So incomplete are our lives
without Him.

Am I on a "spiritual high"? Yes,
indeed! For I've found a "piece of
the puzzle" to my once very
fragmented life. It is the completion
of me. What? No...Not the end of
all my growth. Rather...at this moment
my life makes more sense than ever
before.

And what does this commune with
my God bring? It brings the greatest
of attainments...Peace within. Will
this gift from my Higher Power be
threatened and tested? Yes.
So, I must fellowship with The Almighty
every day...an ongoing, open
communication with much reverence.

Tonight I dance the dance of celebration.
I'll let it "soak in", then begin to share.
Selfishness with the love possible
for everyone is forbidden. So, I
pray for you my friends. May my
spirit of rejoicing, somehow bring
hope for you. In the Son's Love!

She and He

She doesn't always know me.
He knows I'm as hard-headed as him.

She doesn't see to her left side.
He uses "readers", even though
he's had routine surgery.

Her hair is now always disheveled.
He insists on having his hair cut by a
particular barber...in the next town.

She may start singing when the notion strikes.
He has never been able to "carry a note".

Her forte was English and History.
His occupation and research was scientific.

She was always somewhat scared to drive.
He thinks he should still be driving.

She still loves to talk.
He says what is necessary, and a bit more.

She uses a walker and a wheelchair.
He shuffles more and more as time passes.

She sleeps most of the day.
He falls asleep, sitting in the chair beside her bed.

She has found her home.
He is determined to bring her home.

They will never share what they once knew.
Their love continues to surpass any earthly limits.

They made God their Ally and He has protected
their Union.

Someday

My history...the past...hmmm.
Blessings and conflict within.
What has been "the good"?
People. Yes, the people in my life!
What has been "the bad"?
A body chemistry producing inner turmoil.

So, have I learned anything from my past?
Heavens...Yes!! And immensely grateful.
The people...friends, family and strangers.
In one way or another they added to my benefit.
Directly or indirectly they were part of the
formula for faith, hope and love.
The body chemistry. What good could come?
Perseverance, strength, appreciation for what is.

On to the present. Constant situational tests.
All natural and expected in life.
Obstacles. Battles. Sadness. Again, part of
the agenda. God...a steadfast partner.
No parties, grand travels or escapes.
Always the view is of the aged.
Youth has seemed abandoned.

Ok, what's the lesson being taught?
What am I learning in my present?
Security. I watch as those before me
face their next step. The step into the
afterlife. A growing faith produces
an evolving sense of safety. And how
extremely priceless. Much thanksgiving.

Hold on. More has been attained...
both from the past and present.
For real? Yep! And it's good "stuff"!
It resides in my core being. What is it?
Happiness, contentment and peace!
It may not surface frequently...at least
not right now. I must bide time.

The future. What will it bring?
It is not for me to know. Could be
good...could be bad. Optimism...
that's the key to looking favorably
into "the crystal ball". And I believe.
Believe what? This...
Someday I'll revel in the already
acquired happiness, contentment and peace.
In this world? Yes, I truly believe!

Friends Prayers

What is involved in a prayer request? Well, we are asking for people to take note of our situation. This takes a persons', usually a friends' time. Even the split second prayer requires one to cease what they are thinking or doing, put their own affairs on the back burner...just for us. Some may think that is no big sacrifice. But I believe one who truly prays for another is setting aside what may be their limited, precious time. And that is a sacrifice. What else are we requesting? We wish for another to go before their Being of faith and intercede for us. That is a big deal. Our friend is allowing us to be a part of their relationship with their God. That is indeed personal for the one who offers the prayer...all on our behalf. Yes, a prayer may be viewed as the simplest act of trying to help another. But it's not. It's the ultimate. Friends, I want to express my gratitude for your prayers concerning my issues. I feel extremely fortunate to have you by my side. There is much physical distance between us. Also, we may not intimately know each other at this point in our lives. But God's spirit knows no boundaries or limits. And with that fact, prayers are answered. Maybe not to our expectations, but absolutely according to His will. Thank you my Facebook Friends! Much Love, Sara

To Get Mad or To Be Mad

The yell, the scream, the shout...
out loud. Not acceptable. At
least not in public. So, the home
must absorb such intense anger.
The mother, father, brother, sister,
child, pet...all victims of the volatile
expression. Perhaps, the issue at
hand has nothing to do with these
persons. How unfair...what they
must hear...what they must witness.

But the internal combustion, it has to
escape the body trap. Oh really?
Why not "simmer down"? May not
be possible. The temper has worn
thin from constant strain. Maybe
others are blamed. Or maybe it's a
sort of self-degradation that's taking place.

Let's say it's not the fault of another.
What do we have left? Our person.
Our personality. Our thoughts and
emotions. Our coping mechanisms.
Do we feel used by our own beliefs
which sacrifice our humanity? Is it
a reaction to falsehoods we've asserted
on our conscience, leaving a fill of guilt?
Could it be distorted perceptions?

Regardless, we cry out. In silence or heard
by others. Is it wrong that we "let go"?
If it hurts another...we need to "step back".
If it hurts us...we need direction. Yes...
where does this expression of anger lead
us? We are the only person responsible
to make sure it remains safe.

So...to get mad at ourselves. Many times
it's ok. But there are times precaution is
necessary. Don't want to go "overboard".
But again..."getting it out of our system".
We need to exorcise our ill feelings.
What about...to be mad? What I speak of
is the insanity that can evolve when we
"look the other way". When we don't
face the facts that are ever so present.

As for me, I'd rather "throw a fit" in the
confines of my home than aid the growth
of what would develop into a monster.
That's just me. But to be totally honest...
there is a layer that has yet to be peeled.
And the anger that lies within its shield...
it must be faced. But I have a faith...
however fragile...that there will be release.
So, I "plug along". One step at a time.
And make sure I'm as "nice" to myself
as possible, according to my personality.
And onward the walk continues.

My God's Total Control

What more is wanted? So much I have already turned over to my God. Hitting rock bottom, I fervently prayed for release from my bondage. Repeated cries of help are necessary for some nature of hope. I continue to give up my own will power, as I see it serves no real purpose. Understanding, taking action, and reasoning have not befriended me into a state of desirable being. I have no control of decisions others make. Yet those decisions can dictate what will happen to me. So, the issue of fairness does not enter into the equation. Is this another form of relinquishing my all to my Maker? It has to be. There is no other way to view it and remain sane. So, my God seems to be telling me that not only does he want complete control, but he's also allowing others to have control over me. He is not saying that I cannot be my own individual. And I trust he will not put me in harm's way. So this is it. Give it all up. He wants my total compliance with his plan for me. It is no longer my agenda. And then there's the unknown. What is the plan? I suppose if I knew his design, I might try to rearrange, scheme or project my actions. No, my God wants total control. He says "Let me be your all." What can I say? I cannot refuse his offer to take care of me. It makes my body literally sick if hold onto "my way". Do I want to feel the fear that my best intentions produce? Even if my intent is legitimate? No, I want freedom from such severe qualms. So I will wait on my God. His move will be mine. Let others make the judgment calls at hand. My God has control over them. I must totally humble myself and let the chain of events just happen. And let my whole person find an ease of existence. Yes, this is what I want. No longer the futile fight. I will rest on Him and allow His promise of peace to envelop me.

A Broken Bone, A Broken Mind

Stumbling towards the floor.
You know it's coming.
Then a "crack"...a "pop".
It's loud. You know there is damage.

There is immediate help. A person
who relates. A place to go for help...
without a second thought. It is
obvious. Attention is necessary.
There is understanding.

Relief is given readily...without question.
The pain is seen with the naked eye.
A pain that makes sense to all.
It could happen to anyone.
And everyone knows this to be true.

Easing towards torment, you're not
sure when it will reach its greatest
height. Then there's a "click"...a "snap".
It can't be heard. Is it for real? Or
is it "crying wolf" inside?

Hesitant...if not afraid, to ask for help.
Has anyone else experienced such?
The place for aid has an undesirable stigma.
It seems a "test". Can one prove its truth?
Others show reservations...well, not all.

At times "on target" assistance is given.
Other times, a solution is nowhere to
be found. The senses make no sense.
Not all are subject. But probably more
than believed. It may not be evident to
others. And far from comprehension…
even to the affected.

Proposal: A goal for society…
Continue to mend the broken bone.
Dare to mend the broken mind.

A Change of Ways

So to proceed in life, change is inevitable.
That is, if we want our life to get better.
Perhaps find a joy that has gone by the wayside.

A particular change that has to do with everyday
habits. Ugh! Impossible to reverse! So, we shout out
and recoil. But no, that option has already been taken...
resulting in more confusion and anger. Ending in a
feeling of futility.

We think we are incapable of such a huge modification.
And if we look at it as a "whole transformation", we
may not be able to "take the bull by the horns". So, the
change must be piecemeal. Ever so small steps.

A significant change will probably involve a lot of
time. And we, as humans, do not like to wait! But we
weigh the consequences and decide we want to feel
more positive. And we want a relief from our burden.
Therefore, the calendar and clock are not our friends.
At least not right now.

We find that "patting ourselves on the back" is very
essential. An expression of success regarding the
change. We also find that this direct demonstration
of pride helps bide our time, in a firm way. Yes, small
reinforcements.

So, even if the change is a very major part of our daily life, we find that the minute achievements help us entertain the possibility that we may reach our goal. Thus, giving us more power to withstand the "hard points".

With all the work involved with change, we tire. So, it is time to rest for awhile. And the encouragement that the small successes provide, allow us to set the issue on "the back burner" for a period of time. Granted, our rest may not last long. For our mind works overtime. But still there is some rejuvenation. How wonderful.

Soon, we look again at the major change for which we hope. Yes, it can be done! And really, time is on our side. We'll boost our morale by "making over" small attainments. And we'll choose to be around people who have faith in us and take our issue seriously.

So, in essence we can have what we desire if we are willing to work towards the goal. We are strong and we have character. Let's not cheat ourselves of recapturing that joy! Commence!

Battleground

Fighting has been intense.
As with any war...
seeking peace.

Tired. Weary. Weak.
A "white flag" signifying
defeat lures...but not.

Bleeding, lacerations...
leaving so many deep
pronounced scars. Invisible
yet felt...literally.

Heaviness of head and gut.
The weight is of a hazy nature.
A blow. A spear impelled.

Pain...sometimes great
sometimes vague. At times
the longed for reprieve...
supplying surer breath.

Fear magnified past reality.
Unclear, unfounded, warped...
the tremendous apprehension.

This waging of conflict...
where is it? A home?
A country? A relationship?
No. It's all in the mind.

Dad...gone astray!

Unbelievable. Incorrigible. Thoughtless. These words describe the actions of my Dad for the past several days. At least, from my perspective. Earlier today, my foot was ready to be firmly planted down, in order to put an end to these ridiculous antics. Yes indeed, he was taking advantage and assuming to get what he felt was rightly his. That being...his way! As the day wore on, and I enjoyed a conversation with a lifelong friend, my spirits lifted. My foot became a bit lighter. I eventually began to think of times that he had NOT "put his foot down" on me. He'd let things slide. In retrospect, I guess back then he knew "where I was coming from"...all along. Oh, I was disciplined in my childhood and teen years when necessary. But when living at home while attending college, he had to have "looked the other way". He was letting me be me. Give me a break...who just goes out dancing at a club? Aren't libations usually involved? How about..."I'm just going to meet some friends at Bennigan's". No, this wasn't a constant activity of mine...well it wasn't ALL the time. But when I did go out for these "nights on the town" or either "just going over to visit a friend" (whose refrigerator was stocked), I was very liberal in my consumption. Coming home in early morning hours, my parents' bedroom door remained shut. Nothing was ever said. And with the stench that must have reeked...coming straight from my free lodging... my evening activities had to have been evident to these wholesome, God-fearing, Southern Baptist parents. Only once, at 4 am, did I hear my Mother's disturbed voice come from their bedroom..."Where have you been?! We were worried!" Of course, I gave some slurred line of bullshit. And that's all that was said. They let it go. And I'm pretty sure it wasn't my Mother who "let it go". It was my Dad wanting me to socialize, have fun, fall, get back up again...with hopes that I'd enjoy my youth and learn at the same time. And I'm positive many prayers were said behind that closed bedroom door. So, remembering my youth today, I took a different look at my aged Dad. And I review my adult life, how much worry, concern and pain they must have felt watching me battle serious health issues. No, I did not bring those problems on myself. But who welcomed me home when my road would come to the end...yet again? Oh...there's so much my parents have done for me in my lifetime. I have been so blessed and fortunate. And the "foot I'm putting down" continues to get lighter. Yes, I gave my Dad some verbal reprimands today concerning his ways. It is necessary for the functioning of our daily relationship. But am I going to let him be "the child"? Of course. It's "where he's at" in his life. Just like long ago, he knew "where I was coming from". He let me be me. Now, I need to do the same for him. It is my responsibility and privilege as his child.

The Gut

Telling you when it's time. Saying "no".
Saying "yes". Leading in a direction.
Will it benefit? Or will the intuition bring
about discourse and fault? For everyone...
this "spot"...located in the stomach? So...
is it a "physical" member of the body?
It seems to be the case. It's so strong.

Power. Yes, very powerful. It can hurt
the psyche in a fierce manner. Oh...I guess
it also consoles...in its own way. Rather
odd, its' workings. Let's say it is indeed
located in the stomach. It has nothing to
do with the intake of food. Yet, it can
house a stomach ache...much like the
result of overindulgence.

"He's got guts!" One hears this ever so
often. The person to whom it refers is
solid, bold, and fearless. His beliefs,
attitudes and values are threaded with
immense strength. Or...on the other
hand, maybe the individual is thought
to be an "idiot" in a masquerade of
self-proclaimed knowledge.

Addressing the nausea. Yes, a literal
sickness. What causes such? Poor
decisions, taking chances, facing
challenges, bad luck, an elation of
goodness, looking inward, "speaking
out", living life, perceptions of death.
So it goes...on and on...plausible reasons.

"The Gut". Much of what is "voiced"
thus far sheds a negative light on this
part of our "mental make-up". Is that
a "fair shake"? I mean, what would we
do without its help? Yes, it does help...
mostly in an uncomfortable manner.
So, it does get a "bad wrap"? Probably.

How to live without the gut? No way.
It is an indispensable source of common
sense...most of the time. Do we really
want to give up the "good" that comes
with the "bad"? I don't. That's the reason
for this write. To exorcise the present
ill feeling. Hopes to ease the body, mind
and spirit...dodging repulsion.

In time, the gut will calm. Belief that a
serenity will "makes its way" to that
part of self. I tell myself..."It will."
Have to promote optimism. What's
that saying..."Fake it, till you make it."?
Everyday. Everyone. We all have
a gut. At times it will play havoc.
And other times it will guide to safety.

What do we do with such "a rascal" of
our personality? No escapes. No
loopholes. Bottom line...we learn to
live with it..."The Gut".

And The Greatest Is Love

Faith, Hope and Love.
And the greatest of these is love.

The fatherless child screams for
unimaginable attention.
And the greatest is love.

The teen with due baby continues
to "hang out" with the "losing crowd".
And the greatest is love.

The young adult afoot, pushes
an old grocery cart alongside the
busy road. A buggy filled by
food stamps.
And the greatest is love.

The mother of four, sticks a syringe
filled with meth into her bruised arm.
Her neglected children cry.
And the greatest is love.

The respected middle-aged man
seeks to regain his youth by secret
passion.
And the greatest is love.

The wealthy senior citizen disregards
the obvious stresses of his neighbor.
All the while, lounging by his pool...
sipping a cool drink.
And the greatest is love.

The cruel elderly woman curses insanely
at the overworked nurses' aide.
And the greatest is love.

Heavens gates open wide.
ALL who believe are welcome.
There have been faults and failures.
There has been faith and hope.
But the greatest has been love.

Eternity?

I can't see! It's too bright.
My eyes are closed for protection.
There is a burning...it's painful.
What is this? It comes from the sky.
But it's not the sun.

I could look down. But my face
remains in an upright position.
I want to know what causes such
an experience. Is it of this earth?
Is it alien? There is a bit of fear.

What to do? How can I learn of
the cause when the sense of vision
is so impaired? Why is this happening?
Did I do something wrong? Am I
being punished?

So...I decide to listen. What do I
hear? It is very still. Even though
I'm afraid, there is a peace. Again...
what do I hear? Silence. Listen
closer...there is a breath. Who is
this that is in my space?

I begin to feel. I feel with my soul.
I reach upward. Nothing but air.
But I feel something. How can this
be? All the while, my eyes remain
closed. I'm impaired. But I continue
to seek the reason.

With vision weakened, I lower my
head. Once more I hear something. It
is coming from within. It's a heartbeat.
It's my heart. And it guides me to bide
my time.

I begin to bow my head. I decide
to ask. Ask who? I guess I should
ask the light, because that is what seems
to be the essence of this aura.

With head still facing the ground, there
is a reply to my inquisition. It says
"Lift your face towards me, open your
eyes and reach to me with your hand."
Should I take such a chance? I might
be blinded for good. And my hand
might be swatted.

In confusion, my heart and soul begin
to be stirred. There is fright. What
has such power to cause my senses to
be heightened to such extreme?

Even though I'm scared, inside I am
led to follow the instructions. I lift
my head towards the light.
I do not feel the burning, only a
presence...in soft illumination.

With eyes still closed, I choose to
stretch out my hand towards the sky.
I touch and feel. It is soft and smooth.
There are no repercussions to my action.
I decide to slowly open my eyes.

What do I see? I begin to focus. It is
the bottom of a white robe. I lift my
head further. There is a face in the now
easy light. The face smiles.

A hand lowers from the being. The
hand is strong and steady. At the same
time it is gentle. It lifts me to stairs.
One step at a time, I rise higher and higher.

As I ascend, I begin to hear voices. Some
talk, some song. Beauty begins to evolve.
My soul begins to fill with such a desirable
freshness. Could it be? Is this it? All fear
begins to subside.

I then realize...yes, I'm dying. But I'm past the scare. Then death ends and true life begins. I'm sitting on His lap. There is such ease and comfort. I look around. There they are... the others who went before me.

My being is filled with a new joy. No more sorrow. No more pain. Purpose is in place. This is so much more ecstasy than promised. Then extreme, pleasing excitement overtakes me. This wonderful sensation is going to be ETERNAL!!!!!!!!!

An Odd God

Who is this God? I have put my faith in this Supreme Being for over forty years. And still I do not know Him as one would think I should...or at least He seems odd to me. No, not all the time...not by any means. Hmmm...An Odd God. At this very moment I hear praises to Him in song. My heart is moved. The lyrics coincide with teachings of my early life. But they also apply to the here and now...as I've aged. A few of the words teeter somewhat stringent...I just "let be". It is best. For the basic "Word" I grasp firmly. But back to this Odd God. Yes, my God is odd. He is not like others who hold power. Love and grace are the foundation. Bounties. Do other gods give these precious gifts? This Odd God...I met Him when I was ten years old. What? A child approaching such authority on a personal basis? How did I learn of Him? He was the faith of my fathers...and mothers. The story was "handed down". So, it was "a given"? No. A decision on my part had to be made. And for me, my words were "Here I am." The astounding aspect of this experience was His presence. I remember clearly thinking at that instance...He IS real. How simple. Yet, daily I complicate. Again, back to my Odd God. He is available for every human. And He promises an eternal, grand afterlife. Describing the "key"...my Odd God comes in three forms. Like pieces of a pie. I am blessed times three. My God provides a Father...that's one piece. And I can sit on His lap. And my God devised access to His being. How? My Odd

God lived a human life on earth. Experienced pain, was outcast and finally killed to pay for my inadequacies. His Son...Jesus. That's another piece of the pie. And that dead Son...He came back to life. Defeating death just for me...and you! I told you my God is an Odd God. Doesn't make much sense does it? Not to me... but I'm solely human. I can only understand so much. Finally, there's the piece that fills my soul. God in a Holy Spirit. What? That's gettin kinda crazy! Sounds somewhat eerie. But this Spirit...it comforts, consoles, brings joy and peace, provides guidance and "sets straight". The Holy Spirit is the way my God exists inside of me. How peculiar...my God is a pie sliced in three sections! Yes, a very Odd God. Do I really believe this? I have to say "yes" to the skeptics. Not because I'm so sure of myself. But it goes way back to that ten year old child. This Odd God became real...real life. Are other gods as accessible? I mean...really...I was just a kid! What did I know? Well, I heard there was a love. And love sounded appealing. I had something in my favor. I already knew what love was like. I had parents who truly loved me. And then...I was offered more love. I heard this love was necessary for life. My parents' love gave me physical life. Now, this Odd God wanted to give me spiritual love and life. Did I "reach out" for this gift when I first heard? No. In fact, I fought it. Why on earth? Well, in order to receive the love...I had to give my Odd God my heart. You know how "hearts" and "love" go together. Like Valentine's Day. Giving away a heart is not necessarily easy. It is our very essence. So, I had to trust this Odd God to hold my heart. Kinda wild and weird, isn't it? Funny... even though there have been bleak times, I've always known my Odd God was protecting my heart. And my heart...He automatically filled it with His love. And what about grace? Free and unmerited favor from this Odd God. Can you believe that? I still can't. But I'm trying to "get out of my way" and just accept. Honestly, I have a long way to go in receiving such gift. And it's not because He's holding out on me. It's because I keep thinking I have to prove my worth. Oh my...how that goes against my Odd God's plan for my life. It's just so hard to believe...It's all FREE! There's nothing I can do to earn it. I can accept that my God has my eternity planned and paid. But what about me as I live my earthly life? Will I torture myself in efforts to try and try? A senseless act of proof. It goes nowhere. I am a human who has an Odd God. That's it...grace is also very odd. Grace is not of this world. And it can only be provided by the God that already loves me. How is it that I find it easier to accept grace in relation to the unknown...you know salvation, but at the same time find it impossible for my God to readily shower me with daily grace? Perhaps because the grace of salvation is so enormous, and I accept that which I will never understand while here on earth. But I want to understand, and expect to understand grace pertaining to everyday situations and my earthly human form. BUT not to be. I have to "turnover" my heart once more...such as I did for God's love. This time in order to allow myself to feel and know God's grace as I live. It's all so foreign and ODD! Interestingly, I do have to work at learning not to work for daily grace. Ugh...I make it so hard! Love and grace so freely given by a powerful God. Whoa...I have not even mentioned prayer. What does it say? Pray without ceasing? Sounds like I need to get down on my knees! Even so, I must say again...in my defense, my God is an Odd God. But then, I've never been known to be very conventional!

A Last Hurdle?

The finish line...Ahh! Well, life will
go on. But a completion of sorts seems
to be transpiring. It cannot be seen
clearly. But its' presence is definitely
felt. A bit apprehensive...will the
progress vanish in the while? Oh...
please no!

Mind games played over and over...
there's a sense they are dissipating.
Albeit very slowly. As with just about
every good thing. Why thu hell do
things...especially good things, have to
evolve so timidly?

Can't make it be. Can't "jump the gun".
It's a gradual occurrence. But this particular
battle...it's been waging for such a long
time. Weariness, fright, disillusionment...
all very relevant in the fight. But have to
keep the faith. Or so, everyone says.
Yes, I choose that course.

Careful not to let intense anticipation find a home. Due to bring possible disaster. No, there must be "air". A type of vacancy must entertain thought processes. This mind is not "made" of such properties. Always hesitant of the "light-hearted". But then again, humor has readily been present. Fortunate release.

So, tonight...it has not arrived. Will there be irrational fear? NO! That is not an acceptable path. It is forbidden. The detrimental roots which have caused such pain...No More! Is this merely self-talk? Well, right now...at this moment...yes. And that is not lack of wisdom. Rather... self-preservation.

The gut so wants change. It appeals to the brain. But that organ is not yet ready to submit. So, go through the motions. Yes, do what's already been done. It has been a lead. Continue to follow. Doubts... they surface. Even so, there has been a growing strength within. The developing of a stronghold. Hang in there!

Time to no longer linger in the "spell".
That is what it seems...a "hex". Let it go
for now. At least as much as ability affords.
Go about the business of what life should be.
For that is what is desired...normal functioning.
Normal? Well, you know..."the norm".
And with that, I will conclude.

STEVIE ROCKS!!!

Just finished watching the Stevie Nicks "Live In Chicago" concert DVD...again! It's amazing how we as young adults mature into middle-age. This concert DVD was made in 2008. A far cry in audience participation than Stevie's "Live At Red Rocks", Colorado DVD. That performance was during the 1980's. Not only did the people look different in Chicago...no big hair, etc. But the rambunctiousness, screaming, posters, lighters held high were not present in the latter concert. Imagine that!! Swaying, clapping, a few yells and whistles here and there were sufficient to express the gratitude and appreciation for the artist' work. Enough enthusiasm for folks in their 50's and 60's to "get down" and really enjoy themselves. And the singer/songwriter seemed pleased and fulfilled. Of course...she's "grown-up" with everyone else. I first noticed the differences within an audience when I was in my early 20's. A friend and I went to a Kenny Loggins concert at Astroworld in Houston, Texas. The seats on the front rows were filled with middle-aged adults. The rest of us stood at the back...which was good for dancing. As you probably know, Kenny Loggins' songs span many years. During the concert, the people in the front sat conservatively and clapped at the end of the songs. The back of the audience was much more demonstrative. But then the concert neared the end, and Kenny Loggins "pulled-out" an oldie but goodie..."Your Mama Don't Dance". Well, that was all the front row audience needed. They all stood up and began to show signs of movement. Even the men in their khaki golf shorts and Izod shirts! They had not forsaken their "heyday". Today, I don't think I could even stand up through a whole concert... haha. No, I'm satisfied to just sit in my living room watching concerts on the television screen. As long as it is "stereo sound"...and loud. I look back at my younger days, and consider myself lucky to have seen Stevie Nicks in person. So, I'm content. But I have to say...I would rather watch her 1980's concert than the 2008 concert. I'm still young at heart! And I LOVE to see Stevie stompin' around in those mega high heels, shawls and her "gypsy" skirts!

Yes...STEVIE ROCKS!!!

Can't Stop Me!

Eyelids kinda heavy and a bit of a burn.
But a cold washrag will fix that.
Eye drops...Yes!! Can't let them close.
Minutes later, opened wide.

Body feels no strain or pain.
Could walk a mile...well, maybe.
Don't want to sit still for too long.
It is possible that sedation would
approach, even when on guard.
Beginning to numb, I'm safe from
being overcome. I can take anything!

Will I go for a ride in the cool night air?
I've already made a trip to the post office
drop box...that was an hour ago...3 a.m.
My reflexes were fine...as far as I could
tell. It doesn't matter anyway. I'm ok.
In fact, I feel good. No, not grandiose.
I will argue the point, if accused.

Do I know what I'm doing? Yes.
Realistic and practical? Who's to say?
Anyway, what clout would that one
carry? No, I'm just as "right" as anyone
else. Right or wrong...who cares?
If there is concern, it doesn't affect me.

Feeling more and more certain of myself.
I have much to do when light appears.
And I will be ready. Success is on the
horizon. There will be deals made today.
Responsibilities to be carried out.
Carried out with ease and no doubts.

Can I "see through this"? Perhaps.
But I don't wish to look. And I won't.
I want to carry on. Achieve goals.
This is too good. Why come down?
Especially when I don't have to.
Can't stop me! Don't dare try!

A Possibility...hidden in plain sight.

The conflict. The turmoil. The unresolved.
In front of the face? Yes. Ignored? No.
But thought to not be so vital. Now viewed
at the very least, a force which stymies growth,
sanity and security. How has one survived the
chaos this issue has wrought? Pure will power.

So, it's been "discovered". Revealed in a new
light. It's power recognized and given respect.
Others have faced such. Why does it hinder
this soul to such great affect? Don't really
know. But what is known, this being has an
extreme sensitivity. Not a weakness. But
an intense "feel" in many areas of life.

So what to do with this "weight" of strife?
It is thought The Almighty, in whom one has
based their faith, is repulsed with the issue.
Is this a fact? No. But it is what one feels.
This person's God...a loving source. How
come one feels so inadequate with regards
to the fact at hand? Perhaps because the
human element surfaces in their perception.

Time to "deal" with it, as never before. It
will be hard and scary. But there is one...
help, a company that assist in the "dig".
Why now? Why not in the past? So much
has been "overturned". And there has been
peace attained with regards to many other
parts of the life. And yet, it is not finished?

I guess that's it...life is always "alive" and
"living". Growing forward. An evolving
should always be taking place. This is
known. So, on the "right track"? Yes, it
is believed. Answers and calm will come.
Relief and release, if work is steady and
truth prevails in the seeking.

Worthiness, self-acceptance, love at the
core, individual respect, in accord with
the Higher Power, the sought for acceptance
from that Authority. These things...just some
possibilities if the search is firm. No "running
from", no deception within. Honesty must
be the focal point. Completion of inner
peace. Yes.

Growing Up

From them I learned of God. To care for others as
myself.
Their lives are honest and fair.
Dependable and true are their deeds.
Sharing, a treasure...from them I learned.
God they are not.
The secret to my life they do not hold.
Wait. I will not throw away what they give.
And I will not take what is forced.
I will see them as they are,
and accept myself for who I am.

SJB 1991

At The Same Time

I guess it's just considered "life".
I mean, these opposites that attract.
Forget the basic black and white.
There are so many variables to
everyday living. One doesn't
necessarily negate the other. No...
definitely not that simple. Neither
does it mean it's bad. It just is.

So, what am I talking about? Well,
emotions, attributes, attitudes...to
name a few. Give examples...ok.
I am a happy person...in my soul.
But circumstances keep "the happiness"
from having a workable relevance at
the moment. So, I'm happy...but I'm not.

What about security? I have a spiritual
faith that promotes a secure basis.
Yet, I find at times I fear the past, present
and future. I'm scared of my own thoughts
and what they may produce. And to assist
fear in making me miserable...the element
of "worry" is "thrown in". Just downright
unpleasant!

Confidence. I can be so sure of my beliefs
and values...and yet "scream" intimidation.
Yes, I know I'm as important and good as
anyone else. But on the flipside, I question
my worth. Crazy...isn't it? I have a God
who has given me His all...and I accept Him.
But then I question as to whether or not He
accepts me. Quality of faith is wondered.
It can bring about a madness.

And then there's "joy", that is so desired.
Deep down I have a joy in my heart. But
right now joyfulness is just about nil. Am
I fooling myself? Do I just "think" I possess
joy? Well, honestly...there is a joy in my
soul. But it doesn't readily exists in my
everyday life...today. I'm not "counting out"
tomorrow. So, there...there's a bit of my faith.

We all want to be hopeful. At least I do.
What good is it to take a breath, if you don't
have at least have a "speck" of hope? So,
do I have high hopes, or at least attainable
goals? Yes, I do. But right now...that is on
very shaky ground. Again, I claim a trait
that seems to be invisible...even to me.

Then there's love. So much can be said
about this portion of our being. It can be
all encompassing and at the same time very
elusive. I know I have a deep love for God
and mankind. But how much do I really
love myself? Hmmm. It seems as if I
tend to be "short-changing" my own person.
And do I harbor even the slightest inclination
of hate? Love and hate...how can they "be"
at the same time? And yet...

Well, the above are enough examples of night
and day sharing the same hours. We can be
blinded by light or either the darkness can
keep us blind to the facts. Regardless, bottom
line...we can't see. So, as to the "negative"
aspects...what do we do? How do we get rid
of them? Just my opinion...definitely give
effort to reverse direction. But do not get
discouraged or "bogged down" by lack of
quick, positive "about-face".

I believe, for me...happiness, security, confidence,
joy, hope and love will eventually come to full
fruition. Yes, even in the midst of weariness
and uncertainty...I believe...I just know. My
God has made sure the "roots" of these qualities
are based in my inner self. Someday, they will
flourish and show themselves in an outward
fashion. They will be tangible. I will really
"feel" them. Until then, I'll "hang my hat" on
what good does come my way.

And What About Worry?

To seek trouble. Cause chaos.
When in fact the actual travail is
of lesser consequence. What we
do to ourselves while chasing
after security.

You see, while sitting with type
and blank screen...worry magnifies
the real issue. For it becomes a
monster. A threat to sanity. It
weaves in and out of thought and
consciousness. What a waste of
time and energy!

What to do? Laugh! Yes, "draw
straws". "Let the chips fall where they
may." "Throw caution to the wind."
Oh...to be so flippant in the mind.
So, let's duel! Yes, fight for freedom.

This war...let's reduce it to a battle.
More feasible to comprehend what
possibilities of success are "at hand".
That is good. That's the way.
It can be "lighter". Indeed, the show
can be less serious. It might even
begin to be comical.

Let go. What? How on earth?
Don't you know it is life of which I
speak? Don't take it so seriously?
Well, I Never...! What do you expect
out of me? It is how I am made.

But the challenge...change. A fact...
I'm only swirling in a hellish vacuum,
while I try to define and perceive
what is infinitely out of reach. But
what is left...inevitably to attempt to
approach thought in the "minor league".

Damn worry! Flush it! The strength of
its power is only what I allow. I'm in
control. And if wise...I let God be my
guide. For my decision making can
fall very short of sensibility. So, what
of it? What will I do this night?
"Stew" inside? Or relinquish the steady
dose of perhaps, prideful misunderstanding?

I'll end this write somewhat unresolved to
the act of "processing". But it will have
to do. Because it is the best I can do.
So, I say..."Worry, flee from me!" And
hope that the heavens show an act of
kindness, settling my soul.

Excuses

You want to do it.
You don't want to do it.
You want to do it.
You know you shouldn't do it.
But you do it anyway.

Crap! Why cause harm?
That is, if the excuse does lead to pain.
Haven't you felt enough guilt?
But your desires override.
Reality takes a second seat.

So, you try to ignore your senselessness.
Deep down there is a grinding.
You can't run. It is there, even if not blatant.
If you're not careful, it can cause nausea.
So, you quickly try to change your thoughts.

Freshness of bad results due to actions looms.
In the past they have devastated.
And yet, here you are again..."acting out".
Will it ever end? Will you eventually conquer?
Oh, you hope. But the desire to change is stagnant.

It's only a simple excuse. Really?
You're right. At this point it seems innocent.
You're not gonna be troubled by the outcome.
That's your train of thinking right now.
You're in the danger zone!

Again...think about something else.
Don't let it get you down. Not now.
Try to enjoy. But there are so many reminders.
You're no fool. Therefore if you think,
you can no longer fool yourself. Damn!
Avoid in order to escape. So, ending this write.

Just Do It

"Just Say No"...How well did that work?
The issue of its concern survives abundantly.
True. It was said with deep conviction and
hoped to produce "a way out". But the
result of its message didn't make much of
an impact. Again, good intentions.

So, you have an obstacle to overcome.
Implications from others might as well
be stated as: Just Do It. Oh...if it was so
simple. Yes, you've dug yourself deeper
into the mire. But it seems beyond your
control. And deep down, you know that
to be true. At least that's the feeling.

But others. You can't help but perceive
that they are irritated and tired of your
fight. A fight that has thus far been
impossible for you to win. In fact, you've
made no progress at all. So, you shut up.
You suffer in silence. They don't understand.
It's not their fault. You don't even understand.

You're looking for an answer. It is possible
there is help on the horizon. But for now...
you're stuck. And the aid hoped for...will it
even solve the problem? You don't know.
Things are vague. So uncomfortable, you've
grown weary. How long will it last?
It's been ongoing for a year. That is...the
severity. It had been a lesser evil years prior.

"Change. Just do it. Put your foot down.
Try harder. It's not such a big deal.
Others have it much harder. Can't you see?
You're bringing it on yourself. If you'd
just put more effort into your attempts.
Nobody can do it for you. It's up to you."

Damn...you already know the above.
You don't want to be in this pit. It has been
impossible to crawl out so far. Can't they
see? You've tried...and you're still trying.
But they want results. All they can see
is the simplicity of the problem.

So, what to do? First, ask your Creator
for better days. Second, don't turn your
friends into enemies. The basis of their
actions and reactions are only your perception.
And those assumptions could be faulty.

What else can be done to overcome? Well,
look for anything positive and cling to it
with all your might. Try to eliminate as much
of the negative impact as possible. If you
can bring any aspect of the problem into your
corner...do so. Laugh at anything...even if
it's not funny.

Time. Oh brother! Yes, it's going to take
more time. But it will come. Keep striving.
No, it doesn't make a lick of sense...this
crazy mind-set. It is likened to a stone
around your neck...causing you to sink deeper
underwater. But keep the faith. There is
hope. You gotta believe among your unbelief.

Well, all this write...and the stand is still.
The issue...not to be solved tonight.
Not to worry...STOP the worry. Or more
realistically... stop the excess worry. Go
about your business. Just for the moment...
pretend. Pretend, so as to survive. And
people, that's all that can be done...right now.

So Detestable!

I hate it! The power I give such a
fruitless, careless, and somewhat
harmful action. It is besting me!
No, I'm not giving up and I'm not
giving in. But I do find myself so
sickened by its "hold".

Rather simplistic, the whole affair.
That is, if you were to call a flaw that
has been ongoing for over a year "simple".
Indeed, it is complex. It confounds.
So it's simple, yet causes such heavy
disruption? Yes.

It seems a curse. I see the devil laughing
freely at my inadequate attempts to overcome. But who is he...but a bold-faced
coward! So, I won't let the slight of spirits
interfere with my hopes of prevailing.

This "thing". It is rather silly...in a fashion.
But its' repercussions are potent. It leaves
a trail of self-doubt and dismay in its wake.
Oh...and regret. Yes, a "pounding" on the
mind, body and soul...leaves remorse.
I can do better. Can't I?

So, what can I do different? It seems I've
tried everything to seek a "fair shake".
But wait. There is an avenue that is
presenting itself...its new and different.
Maybe it will hold the key. Although...
I have to remind myself there is no control
over the timetable.

Repulsion comes to mind. Sounds quiet
agonizing. Well, it is. And the heart is
weakened by its strategy to secure
power. What? Power is involved? Well,
it does seem to have a place in the equation.
I GIVE it power. I don't really know how...
but I do. It will take some unraveling to
make headway. Let's get going!!

What? Sit still? Be calm? Try to relax?
Just how in thu hell is that gonna happen?
I'm tired of this "time" thing. On with it!
Ok...so, you say I'm being too hasty. Well,
considering the amount of my life that it
has consumed, I don't care what you think!

Right. I gotta "settle down". Throwing
bricks at you or God will only make the
matter worse. And of course, I have to
stop belittling my efforts. For I have
given it my all. Perhaps more prayer?
Yes, I should think.

So, in a sense, we're back to the waiting
game. Well, I guess that'll have to do.
I mean...there is no other choice. Yes...
I can make moves in trying to uncover,
reveal and then change. But alas, I still
have to stop looking at the clock. Just
think, if I could stop "wondering when"
and honestly "let go"...resolution is sure
to happen.

God, it's me. You own every minute of
my day. Help me to acknowledge that
fact. I'll do my part. Help me to let you
do your part. Remove my fear, insecurities,
and poor judgment. And take my clumsy
hands off of your business. Amen.

The other night...Nightmare

A mixture. No, not a recipe to eats.
Not a combination of chemicals
entered in a science fair. Nothing
desirable was produced.

So, what were the ingredients?
Mania, extreme obsessive-compulsive
thoughts and acute anxiety. Resulting
in a detonating, yet quiet "mind calamity".

Yes, all the combustion was internal.
There were some serious considerations
of irrational actions. Not to worry.
None of direct self-destruction. Instead,
ideas that could lead to possible danger.
Thankful in hindsight, enough sensibility
manifested itself within.

Such fright was present. Fears of lack
of control. The unknown of what
would take place inside the weighted
head. Would it explode? No, it would
remain a continuous heavy burden.
Thinking...never to cease. A fearful,
miserable state. Weak and sickened.

The hours passed. By daylight, a decision
to intervene had been formulated. But
by advice from an individual who had
just woke, the approach to the quandary
was negated. Wisely. Instead, a sound
notion came...which lured the body to a
necessary day of sleep and rest. Fortunate.

I Want an Angel

An angel. Yes, something from Heaven.
A Being to answer questions. Make conversation.
A companion who always "hangs around".
Giving out unique, desirable gifts.
And all these attributes...unconditional.

Do I have to deserve? Must my choices
consist of the "right" decisions? Am I not
to falter in my daily walk? Do my words
always have to sound of clarity? Does my
mind have to be on positive course?

My...what if the above qualifications must
be met? Doesn't look too good. I mean...
I stagger. I'm weak. I choose inappropriately.
I speak...and the words have no substance.
My mind goes "round and round".

I want an angel. But should I be allowed
such pleasure and security? It's of the
Bible. And I'm not that well-versed in
scripture. Oh...I guess others consider
angels coming from different realms. But
I choose to believe my upbringing. That
source being "The Good Book".

So, what to do? Wait a minute...
I do recall portions of holy talk. And
those words say something about a
sacrifice. What? Something took my
place? Somebody paid the price? You're
telling me the bounty is free?!

Well, I want what's offered! I'll take it!
I can actually have an angel? All mine?
A friend from above. Something to
watch and guard over me. A presence
that will guide. For real? What's the catch?

You say surrender? Hmmm. I don't know.
Sounds kinda fishy. So, surrender what?
MY WILL?!!! You gotta be kiddin me!!
I can't just live "on a whim". I have
important decisions to make. How can
I do that if something else is in control?

Trust is the key? That's what you're
saying? I'm not sure. I doubt ALOT!
You say that's ok?! Well...so how do
I trust enough to make it be? It doesn't
take much? I just say "Here I am."?
That's all the trust I need in order to
surrender? Ok. I did it. I surrendered.

Feels pretty good. I feel kinda complete.
Thank you. NOW...where's my angel?
What did you say? Oh...ok, I'll shut up.
I'll let you speak. I'll just listen. Is this
part of that surrendering stuff? Believe so.

It's been awhile. Hey, I sorta see something.
It's a light. It's showing me the way.
Where are we going? Ok...I'll just follow.
There's something in the air. I sense safety.
Who's there? Ok...I'll be still. Funny...
an image is appearing. Well, I'll be!
I've Got Me An Angel!!!

New Year's Day in Our Neighborhood

I was very lucky growing up. I lived in a "real" neighborhood. Friends borrowed sugar and flour from each other. Barbecues and fish fries. We shared vegetables from each other's gardens. So happened that most of us went to the same church. There was swimming and skim boarding in the ditches after a big rain. Plus, one time my neighbor and I caught enough crawfish to sell to the local bait shop. We each profited about 75 cents. Our front yard was the football field and baseball diamond. And we had a concrete slab which was the perfect basketball court. I believe one reason we bonded so well was because most of us were "transplants" from another city or state. My parents being from Arkansas. BUT...let me get this straight...I am a Native Texan! And proud of it! But all along I had a divided allegiance...Texas, my home and Arkansas filled with relatives. At any rate, since a lot of our families "lived off", we neighbors shared many holidays together. It's a tie...the best food is at neighborhood get-togethers and also at church Wednesday Night Supper Meetings, each month. Well, getting on with the New Year's story. Our neighborhood had a big feast at the home next door. I guess I was about a senior in high school. We had all kinds of holiday and New Year's Day food. My next door neighbor's mother would always make yeast rolls...that were delicious! We'd eat and eat, visit, watch football games, be enthused with each other's Christmas gifts and catch a nap sitting up. Anyway, that particular year the yeast rolls were especially good and I had my share. Well, I had finished and went and sat on the couch ready to watch a ballgame. Soon after I sat down, I began having trouble breathing...kinda mildly gasping. Scared Me! I went in where the women were still sitting at the table visiting. I told my mother..."Momma, somethin's wrong. I can't breathe very good". It didn't take her long to come to a conclusion. She said..."How many homemade rolls did you eat?" I said..."I guess about seven." Then she, in reply... "Well, Sara! The yeast is probably still rising in your stomach!" I said... "Well... what do I do?" I don't remember her reply, but she wasn't too concerned. There I was dyin', and my mother was sharing recipes!! I think she did tell me to walk around for awhile before I sat down. Which I did. Even so, when I took my seat again...I could still feel the effects of my gluttony! I was still a bit nervous about the whole "food affair". But I soon got over it. Thereafter, I used better judgment when eating yeast rolls or really "yeast anything"!

So my friends, as we overindulge this year...Beware of the homemade rolls!

DEAR FRIENDS, HAPPY NEW YEAR'S 2014!!!

Why Keep Fighting?

Why continue to fight when
we continue to lose? Because
deep down there still lies some
hope.

It's tiring. You know that.
I also know. Physical or
mental it tears and wears.

Coming up with the same
detrimental results, one would
think that a lesson would have
occurred. But not always.

It's senseless. How foolish the
actions. Are we all actually
fools? I don't think so. But
the facts are facts. I wonder.

Let's return to the fight.
Are we giving it our all?
We think so, because at times
there seems to be nothing left.

Are we asking for help?
Yes, at times. And then there
are the long periods of trying
"our way" alone.

Is what we're fighting for, worth
the effort? By all means. That
should be enough to somehow
help us overcome. But it's not.

What is it? What are we fighting?
Pain, fear, complications, death?
Does its' severity propel more
fervor? In most cases.

So we keep fighting. It is the
only thing to do. We want change
or cure. We want to win. It's innate.

Two steps forward...one step back.
One step forward...two steps back.
Regardless, we continue to tread.

And that hope. It keeps us turning.
What would be our fate if it were
not bedded in us? Let's not go there.
Let us continue to grasp and clench
it tightly in our fist.

Hope for the present and hope for
the future. Yes, it can "turn the tide".
And we grow. We "know", like we've
never known before.

So, why keep fighting? A positive
state could be revealed. That change…
that cure. Yes, say a prayer…
and keep hoping.

Mild Mania

Tired, weary...but the body says "go".
Sleepy but wide awake.
Aching but numb.
Physical strain to speak aloud.

Thoughts are of good judgment...
so one thinks. Goals of a certain
bedtime go by the wayside.
The end to the night/early morn is
likened to the child resisting sleep.
How the clock is hated.

Reasons for activity are justified...
justified by manipulation.
Music loud. Drives in the dark.
New causes to stay awake. Usually,
respectable tasks...but the hour is
not acceptable...so another would think.

Medication is taken at the appropriate
time...Except the one that holds the
sedative. Mind games are played.
Hours pass. Finally it is taken...
out of fear. A fear of truly extreme
fear. For this medicinal unit holds
psychosis at bay. Fortunate that this
reality is still realized.

Sleep finally takes place in an upright
rocker. Maybe on top of a bedspread
if the body screams. But sometimes
sleep is "beat"...and the daylight appears
without the eyes ever closing.

Trudging through the day in exhaustion
becomes customary. If the fight has
not yet ended, there are periods of
high anxiety due to bizarre physical
sensations and the thoughts of lack
of control. It seems this would deter
such senseless decision making.
But not so. One knows actions are
not wise. Even so...

It may "go on" for days or months.
How long can the body take the
torture? A perplexing and ironic
state. Instead of "rest for the weary",
one views rest as the adversary.
Why? Body chemistry...usually
passed on from generations.

The mind...so complex. Common
sense vague. Calculations riddled
with mistakes. Reasoning hampered.
Sight blurred. Walk staggered.
Yet, the writing continues...for now.

Treasure Box

The past carefully taken out of the box can
be pleasant to the present. Then placed
again into the box, as to not alter the future.

The "good stuff", it can never be changed
or stolen. It can be kept forever, despite
any adversity.

Your time in that box will always be mine.

SJB November 4, 1993

Risky Living

How easy to speak when people want to hear.
How sure are our steps when they walk with
conformity.
Dreams which others see are easier to attain.
But what did I need to say?
Where did I want to walk?
What are dreams if they belong to someone else?

SJB 1993

The Ghost Behind

Either waking or having never
gone to sleep...it's just another night.
Pitch black...nothing can be seen.
Quiet...except for snoring across
the hall.

Older sibling laying in the bed beside.
Doors locked. Peaceful neighborhood.
No intrusion ever experienced. Safe.
And yet, fierce fear pervades...every night.

Dare to get out of bed? The spread is some
security. Just some. Is there something at
my feet? I see...but is it really there?
Something's there. I have to get away.
I want to jump up and run. But frozen.

There's security in the other room. They
are always there. I think...I think...I grow
more and more fearful. Terror is beginning
to grow. I must "make a dash for it"!

Quickly my feet hit the cold tile floor.
I'm a sure target. I have to be fast. I have
to reach and feel forward...making sure not
to run into anything. I am totally blind.
Anything can happen. "Scared" is not the
word to do justice.

The doorway out is already opened.
But I must turn a knob to access security.
I fumble in the darkness. Open and enter.
The snoring is now loud. Each step, I
pray I will not collide into harm.

I finally "make it" to where I can touch.
Touch the safety net. Whispering, I
repeat what is said every night. "Momma,
I'm scared. Let me get in bed...please."

Reluctantly, room is made. There is not
much space...the bed isn't very big. I slide
in. What relief...I'm safe and sound. At
an earlier age, I'd find my way to the middle.
But I can barely fit on the edge now.

But I'm so secure. I drift off. I'm kinda
aware of being carried back to my bed.
By now, I'm not an easy haul. How they
must tire and be irritated with my company.

Too old. The fears should be in the past.
But scared all the same. What is it? What
am I afraid of? I don't really know. It doesn't
have a face. It doesn't make a sound. Nothing
touches me. And yet, I'm terrified.

Knowing my days are surely numbered…
I "strike a deal". A toy for refrainment.
A yo-yo. Yes, a yo-yo becomes my
security blanket. So much so…I place
it under my pillow at night. Amazing…
somehow "it works". No more nightly
walks.

And so years pass. Many years. There is
stress. Apprehension sets-in. I find
myself avoiding "giving up the ghost".
I don't want to be vulnerable. I'm not
really scared of the dark…but there is
a fear. A fear that prohibits easy surrender.

I don't know what it is…this fright.
But it must be "uncovered". And there
is a certain amount of fear in knowing
the unknown. It is said…there has been
a trauma at some time. But I have no
idea what it could be. Was it so terrific
that it hides from consciousness?

As I seek to find reason, I must remember
it is a "ghost" from the past. I AM safe.
Rationally, there is nothing of which to
be fearful. Whatever is rooted…it is of
long ago. I have to keep this fact in mind
as I "bring out" the force which seems so
overwhelming. And maybe buy a yo-yo.

I Feel Good!

I feel good...and I'm gonna
go with it. The future...just
looking into the night, no
further. Besides, that's all
that's guaranteed. So, natures'
darkness shines bright!

Just hours ago, the feeling was
somewhat down. There was
fear and a dark doom. Striking
the senses, my person hit me
hard. Why be so mean? Was
the emotion reality? Yes and no.

What made the difference between
what was and what is at present?
A claiming of gifts. Yes. I said...
"I'll take that!" What was it? A
faith. Faith that can be elusive.

Is it my fault that I'm not happier
more often? Sometimes. But
other times it is out of my control.
Can't be helped. But wait...
speaking of help...there can be
help on the way! And tonight
angels appeared!

Were the angels in the form of people?
No. Were they words in The Book
of Life? No. What then? How
did the about-face occur? Let me
tell you...it was His presence!

Yes, the Holy Spirit. No. I'm not
"goody-goody" or a bold witness.
Even so, my God shone in my
home. A much needed visit.
Again, right in my home...right
where I live. He came to me.

Am I on a type of spiritual high?
Perhaps...kinda. Is it real?
Most definitely! He is the God
of my Mother who is sleeping
in the nursing home. He is the
God of my Dad resting in his
bed...just down the street.

What do I owe my God? Why...
my heart and soul. How do I
know this is what He wants?
Because I learned of Him from
the Mother sleeping and the
Father resting. How grateful.

Should I put such stock in my
parents' beliefs? I choose to.
For their lives have been examples
of what a spirit of heights exists.
And it is on a level plane. Consistent.

What has been the product of their
faith? It has been an outpouring of
love for me...all my life. How
fortunate I have been. Forever I
am responsible to share what they
have given me.

So, tonight I feel good. Tomorrow
is another day. No one knows what's
in store. Should I be wary? Only if
I let doubts creep in. Well, there'll
always be doubts. But I speak of
doubts that hinder the "feel-good".

I write. I express. I let you know...
it can be yours too! It's all for the
taking. Hope. That's what it is...
hope and love combined to make
a grand and ultimate gift. A "present"
given by The Almighty! And
I accept!

A Glimpse of A Mind

Well, we all have one. It can even be
called..."A mind of our own". So different
from one another we are...thank goodness!
Everybody made from a unique pattern. And
I believe the brain, which in a sense "holds"
the mind, can be wacky as all get-out!! (Boy...
that was a Southern statement!)

The carefree is never totally free. But it lives
a life of comfort, with regards to thought
processes. Even so, that person may be struggling
with severe physical troubles. Or perhaps, issues
involving relationships are tumultuous. And
what about money? The "carefree needy". It is
so evident that everyone has a cross to bear.

Looking at the "cross" of the mind. Does it
race endlessly? No reigns can hold it back.
It goes on and on...causing immense havoc. "Just
put your mind to it." "Get a grip." Some statements
made by those whose senses do not dwell so
tightly inward. An impossible task for the
afflicted brain which runs rampant.

What about sorrow? A head that holds such
grief that it is literally impossible to physically
move. Yes, frozen. A deer in the headlights.
The pain associated...unbearable. One feels
as if no other understands. Where does this
person go for comfort? Many times...nowhere.
Just existence into eventual numbness.

Do it. Do it again. Then do it again...and again.
Never the finish line. Hands never clean, even
though there is a thorough use of soap. So weird...
some think. It can be funny. And at the same
time it rips daily tasks. Not to mention thoughts
that return forever and more. Never to cease.

Flying high! Grand ideas! Great feats!
The body never rest, as the brain works in a
form that makes so much sense...to the
person who's doing the thinking. Not to
worry, they've "got it together". Such progress.
Overachieving in every respect. Then the body
begins to wilt, as physical respite has been nil.
No sleep for this brilliance. Until...the bottom.

Perspiration...so cold, then hot. Will I scream out
profanity in this quiet social setting? Am I going
crazy? The heart beats heavy. Such fear of loss
of control. What is this that possesses me?
I can't breathe. I'm dizzy. I feel faint. And all
this ridiculous state stems from a fear? Sometimes
I see the cause, and other times there is no reason.

Distortions within. Hard to define a passing feeling of unreality. Incapable of allowing a human of significance to get close. Perhaps trauma suppressed. Abandoned, all the while holding hands with another. A hollow center...could be. Self-destruction so enticing. But why? Have to dig. What is the reason for such anger? Makes no sense. My, what a reaction to something so small. Who am I?

Please. Can some sanity surface for good will? Allow this mind to float, yet be grounded. Open the window to sunlight. Will peace be afforded among the cruel setting? How one hopes. How one pleads. Yes, there will be a day of reckoning for the enemy. The monster will lose his vision and falter. Being stripped of all power, he will quietly fade and no longer be. And yes, there will be rest while here on earth. Thanks Be To God!

When Our Hurting Irritates Others

We may feel low from something, be it big or small. The feeling is very real. We can't run or hide. We must face the occurrence or predicament. Other people may or may not be directly involved in the situation. Say we are "in it alone". But we express our thoughts and moods to friends and family. Let's say this particular problem has been ongoing. We feel as though people are tired of hearing us. And possibly, rightly so. Are we whining? We don't think so. But are we the ears of the listeners? One may say..."Wait a minute. If they are true friends they'll stick beside you." There's the difference. Who said just because they have tired of our story, that they don't "have our back"? Again...the pain is real. But the listeners may feel action or change, on our part, should have already been taken. They may feel depleted from rendering suggestions...suggestions not tried. Or maybe we have never ever really "heard" the options they are sharing. We are so self-absorbed at times. But what if the suggestions honestly don't apply? What to do? They have tried to help us and we are still stuck in our quandary. We know these people will not leave us. But they just might "shut the door" on our present state. Do we blame them? I don't think so. They have the right to stay sane, regardless of our needs. We may be seeking professional counsel. But we want our loved ones to "feel" with us. We want to get more and more of it "off our chest". We want the problem to be solved. But we are "going in circles". And our friends and family are beginning to see the "circle" we have drawn. Perhaps it's time we just "shut up". But that will leave us all alone. Yes, we have been seeking help from God...and will continue. But we still ache. And the frustration is still present. So, we are by ourselves in the matter. This is when it is absolutely necessary that we like our person. If not, self-hate will permeate even further. Just maybe in solitude with the issue, all the counsel and suggestions will align with a "train of thought" in our mind. Hopefully, guiding us to a solution to the problem and easement of pain. Ok...so when? That usually can't be determined. But it definitely won't happen if we don't "move" first. Being stationary is not an option. This is when we "try and try again". A certain amount of action, be it positive, can diffuse the intensity of the hurting. Why? Because we are "acting" with hope on our side. Back to our friends and family that we have "worn out". They have probably recuperated from our "incessant spouting". We may divulge some of our progress. In fact, they may even inquire. "Keeping to ourselves" on the particular issue, does not mean we kept other aspects of our life from dear people. It doesn't mean that we have continually put on a "brave face". No, our people know we are still struggling. They may indeed be "feeling our pain". Even though they could take no more of our talk, we have probably been in their prayers. This touches on the quality of our friends, family and our relationship with them. So, we really got on our loved one's nerves. Maybe even made them mad. I'll break away here...I'm truly blessed, my people are still around! I hope you to be as fortunate.

Here You Are, At Middle Age

No need to incessantly promote your point of view...
it comes naturally in your actions.

You no longer need to have others understand
"where you're coming from".
You feel positive about the direction you're headed.

Looking at your past, you may wish you wouldn't
have done some things.
But you can put "regretting" in the rear view mirror,
if there is unnecessary remorse.

You have learned from innocent mistakes...
to the point of not repeating those same costly errors.

Asking "why" does not seem as important as it once
did.
You've learned that some things "just are".

Once differences with others brought divisions.
Now you grab hold of things you find in common,
and let relationships grow.

At one time, pain brought on a "flight to escape".
Since you've overcome past sufferings, you know you
can prevail again.

You can laugh at yourself and the blunders you make.
Because what you do is not as important as you once
thought.

You can love easier.
Now, you are aware of how hateful feelings can
destroy the good life.

You see that choices can determine future happiness.
At the same time, you accept that you can't control
what is meant to be.

Being satisfied does not mean you are "just settling".
It means you are content with what your life is all
about.

Here you are at middle age.
So far, problems arose and solutions were found.

Now, what's on your horizon?
Actually, you don't know for sure.

Just let what you've learned in the first part of your
life...
be used as strategy in commencing into your precious
future.

Reckless Revelations

No, not speaking in the Biblical
sense. That chapter of The Word
which can invoke warranted fear.
Instead, the here and now. Although,
some may think we are already in
the predicted turmoil. But let's just
look at the revelations on our trek
to "self-actualization".

A dulled frequent fear makes its' home
in the body. Such an unkind guest.
We have fought and sought. And the
battles continue to weave in and out of
our lives. One can say… "Just a part of
life." And that is so. But apprehension that
produces panic, worry, indecision, guilt,
nausea...it's got to go.

You say...Why such dreary talk? Must
you analyze every aspect of your being?
In response...It comes naturally. For
what that's worth. A downfall? Perhaps.
Regardless, it exist. So be it.

About this...what is being called "reckless
revelations"...so, they bring anxiety.
The desperate seeking for absolution.
Yes. The invasion by a sense of doom.
Oh...maybe that's too extreme. But it
does not feel good. And there is concern
for the future. Why? Because the past
is unresolved. It wasn't purposely avoided.

I used the word "dulled" to describe the
fear. Well, it's also a developed ex-
communication with self. Does it always
loom with such force? No. But it "hangs
around" just enough to pester. That is,
when it's not trying to devastate.

Ok. What of the revelations? Scared of
what will be found? Why? Is it bad?
Does it hold a sort of evil power? A
power too strong to keep sanity? Well...
time will tell. But I'm optimistic...
as much as this depressive personality
affords.

And they are "reckless"...these revelations.
So easy to assume such. Magnifying
what hasn't even happened. Bringing
strife to what could "not be". So what of
it? What is it that is feared? That's just
it...it's the unknown. Not outside, but
within. A darkness, a trap, a suction.

Does it revolve around the total of life?
Right now, yes. But "working" on the
problem is taking place. So, there is faith.
In fact, there is a belief that relief will
surface as the delving takes place. Yes…
chances are being taken. Invisible chances.

And what will come of tomorrow? Will the
blunt suffering caused by what has yet to be,
override daily business? Well, lately…it has
"won out". Not due to weakness of the mind.
Instead…appropriate, limited understanding.
For if cause were known, problem…solved.

There is a belief that questions will be answered.
There is hope that acceptance will take place.
There is security provided by the Maker…
even if not readily felt. No, the process cannot
be avoided. Toiling is a must. Nothing comes
free…except The Way. And for the moment,
that will suffice for adequate survival.

"Houston...we have a problem."

"Houston...we have a problem."
The wiring...it's screwed!
We need help fast!
We're rattled, scared, confused.

It seems impossible to solve.
But that kind of thinking won't help.
We gotta know it will "straighten-out".
What to do? We don't know...yet.

"Yet"...yes, I said "yet".
So, there is hope? A glimmer.
Maybe it will grow into an answer.
And with that answer, bring change.

A "fix". May be temporary for now.
But it will get us by.
Can it really happen? I think so.
The crash...possible to stop.

Meanwhile, up here in space...
How to stay sane and calm?
Breathe deep. Be easy on self.
Cooperate as best we can.

Don't punish if results are not ready.
Keep working...surviving at the least.
There is a home base.
We will return to earth safely.

Steady. Believe. Have faith.
Parts can be rearranged to suit.
Still don't know how. Frightening.
Fear..."Halt"! There's no room for you.

There are those helping us.
They are seeking what we can't see.
Allow them to aid. They also sweat.
They intensely desire positive outcome.

"Houston...we have a problem."
We know there will be relief of anxiety.
Keep that fact in mind. Keep it!
Safety. Lord, keep us safe.

While we wait...try to relax.
It may seem impossible, but we can manage.
Throw away terror as we know it.
And most of all...pray without ceasing!

Progress...and yet...

Such progress through the years, and yet a significant amount of ignorance still prevails. What am I talking about? Well, what I usually am inclined to focus on... mental health. You say..."Get over it!" But I can't help but be persuaded, it is "where I live". Not that I don't try to make other aspects of my life have "life". But the overwhelming conflict...how it throttles. Are we always only going to allow what we see...what we see in the physical sense? Please people! Open your eyes! And when you do, open your hearts. That may be it. The way to see the effects of mental disorders is through the heart. Could be. Today I went for a breast biopsy. I was treated like a queen. There was compassion and understanding. My issue was "real". It wasn't conjured up in my head. The facilities where I was a patient were up to date, immaculately clean, hospitable, and there was a "positive vibe". The doctors and nurses gave much credence to what I had to say. I was taken seriously. And for living in a rural area, driving only half an hour was exceptional. As I write, I realize there are many superb mental health clinics and hospitals in our country. BUT...not enough. And they are "the exception". I speak these words from past and present experiences. So, why? Why is the overall quality of mental health care lacking in the positive? Well, just look at us. We act immature, irrational, suspicious, radical, odd, ridiculous...for starters. And we seem to constantly "shoot ourselves in the foot"...sometimes on purpose. We lie. We threaten. We steal. We cheat. We "get loud". We can "get physical". We wander aimlessly within ourselves. We refuse help. We don't take our medication as directed. Some of us appear physically "out of the norm" with society. And dirty... some of us are very unkempt. On the other hand, some of us "blend right in" with the world. Basically, we don't make sense...to the average person. Who wants to invest patience, time and money for what are many times futile efforts? Who? The few who have an insight into our minds. The few who can take uncalled-for abuse. The few who find the challenge appealing. The few who know disappointments are going to be numerous...but don't let that fact deter. The few who simultaneously have a thick skin and a soul of love and compassion. So, there are some? Yes, there are some who are attracted to us...and want to help. Do I sound as if I'm ostracizing "us" with personalities equal to a dreaded plague? Yes. Is it fair to take such a stance? Maybe so...maybe not. I'm just speaking for myself and from my experience. My friends...I'm talking about "my" friends, I realize most of you accept me for who I am. And I am extremely grateful. But what about my "brothers" who also carry the weight of mental disorders? Some...outcast, threatened, disowned. Let me go back to my experience in the hospital today. Fact: Women who have breasts are in the majority. Well, a given...easy to "relate". Fact: A woman who paces up and down a hallway, muttering curse words with a glazed, distant look in her eyes is in the minority. While the woman who has concerns of the breast is taken "underwing", the "crazy" woman is avoided. And much of the root to the avoidance is fear. Fear...of the known, fear of the unknown. Not to overlook those who have an informative grasp of mental illness, many people "chalk up" mental disorders to the affected having "brought it on themselves". And in some ways that is accurate...BUT people...that can be part of the particular disease. So, what to do? How to bring mental health care up to higher standards? Knowledge. Learn why your aunt gets hysterical. Learn why the neighbor is a recluse. Learn why the stranger in the department store restroom washes and rewashes their hands. Learn why your child continues to have inappropriate outbursts of anger. Learn why the man lives under the bridge. Learn why the young adult resorts to sticking a needle in his arm. Learn why the woman continues to be a "punching bag". Learn why people cry when there is no obvious reason. Learn why some things that are "not there" are "seen". Learn why some people hear music when there are no instruments being played. Learn why the wife continues to "come up" with ailments. Learn why the husband silently retreats to a dark room desiring only the company of a television... night after night. Learn why the teenage girl never has an appetite. Oh...I could go on and on. You get the gist. Thing is...twice last month I had to travel close to two hours to get to a mental health facility. It was Not "The Hyatt". Fellow patients included a young girl who ate pencils, a man with hair dyed the colors of a rainbow and two "streakers". Not an unusual psychiatric hospitalization. We had one psychotherapy group a day. And it lacked depth. Some days we were also able to go to the activities room for an hour. The rest of the time we sat, stared, stewed, worried, watched television and some plotted. There were workers who truly cared and were competent. And then there were others...not so. Stabilized somewhat, I was discharged without having made true significant progress. Only to return in worse health two weeks later. I have to say I did make some discoveries about myself which could benefit my well-being. But there were no real "tools" with which to work towards a difference. So, it was a band-aid. With hopes that outpatient services would deliver the needed help. Again, speaking only from my position, there are no services available to meet my present needs. Oh...I travel an hour every other week for one hour of therapy. Sometimes every week. And I see a doctor once a month for twenty minutes. Well, enough of my complaints...but justified. Once more... back to the breast biopsy. My surgery was scheduled immediately. And the results will be known as soon as possible. Why...of course, it's tangible. It is of the physical nature...could affect life and breath. But what about the mental? The endless dark terror, torment and anguish not equaled. And unfortunately for some, it does stop the physical beating of the heart. So where do we go from here? We have to move forward in treatment for mental disorders. It affects more and more people every day. What will it take? Let's not go there. So, again...knowledge. It begins with learning. Not being afraid to learn. Maybe you are "one". One who inside is hurting. Maybe you don't know the name of "it". Learn...you are not alone. Reach out for what help is available. And let's all pray for much needed progress in care. A "feeling"...lying in the pit of your gut. A "thought"...trapped in the maze of your mind. Are you willing to venture? You better be...for the sake of sanity.

Come Ride The Ride
(From mania-riddled 1990's)

Sitting empty, I felt used. A whirlwind took hold for three months. So much accomplished of which I know not. With its departure I was left exhausted and destitute. Next, my home was a partially opened grave. Seeing light and a possible way out, only on the brightest of days. After two months I was able to climb out. I now sit across from the graveyard. Contemplating my survival and the role of my existence, I carefully glance at a nearby road.

SJB January 28, 1992

Depression

A thought trapped in a maze.
A thought which will not answer the question.
Only fear surfaces as the purpose for breath.
Fear deserved for thought.
Suicide in which despair does not die.

SJB April 24, 1991

Take It Easy!

On A Much Lighter Note!! YAY!!! (And this is for those of you who have been reading what I've been posting recently.) Back in 1985, I was relaxing in one of Beaumont, Texas' well-established "resorts" for a period of 3 months. "The Nut Hut!" At any rate, one day during "music appreciation" we were each given the name of another "vacationer". We were asked to look through the vinyls and pick out a song which we thought applied to them. Loving music so well, I thought...This is great, I'm sure I'll know just the appropriate song to choose. I don't remember what I picked out for the other "vacationer". But I definitely remember what was picked out for me. My roommate had my name. Now...my roommate was a 19 year old girl who had an affinity for cocaine and a truckload of radical emotions. What could she, in all honesty, possibly know about me? Here's the song she picked out for me..."Take It Easy" by the Eagles. When she explained why she had picked it out, she quoted the lyrics..."Don't let the sound of your own wheels drive you crazy". I immediately thought...What Thu Hell? Just where is this chick comin' from? It took years for me to understand and to "get it".

GO FIGURE!!!!

And Trust?

What do I trust?
My gut? Not all the time.
For sometimes my stomach
is queasy. Although my
physiological instincts can
guide...they do not guarantee.

What about my mind?
Do I trust my well-being to thoughts?
Hell no!! Too much ambivalence.
Back and forth. Back and forth.
Bringing the "fear factor" to its
greatest heights. No security whatsoever.

Physical strength to provide protection.
Is that what I trust? Oh my...how the
form can show weariness. A "drain"
on what was once a youthful, energetic
shell...yes, that's what the years have
brought. So, I can't say that my physical
being can be a sure safety net.

My emotions? OH NO!!!
Don't even go there! Sensations that
are rocky and faint can't be trusted.
Sometimes crying, sometimes laughing.
Feelings...they have a huge target
plastered on their back. I'm not putting
my welfare in their hands.

Do I trust other people to "see me through"?
Well, many times the refuge they offered
was adequate...and more. Forever grateful.
But they are not always predictable. And
who's to say they are going to "be there"
when needed? No. Not putting my trust in
the human element.

What about the spiritual? Do I find my
spirit to give me fortitude? Sometimes.
But its' depth depends on my amount
and quality of faith. If I resort to rely
on my own ability to trust...I'll surely
fall prey to deep apprehensions.

What about a power greater than myself?
Well, the spiritual and a basic faith is
intertwined with that concept. So, do
I trust myself to a God? I do. Why?
Because years ago, for fleeting moments
I "let go" completely and a safe bond
was formed.

Am I really gonna let this be my source
of sanity? Yes. When looking at all
the other options...it is the only one
that surpasses what "could be"...
what "ought to be". I trust this God.

What did I say? "I trust this God."?
Why? It seems so silly to claim such.
Am I throwing sensibility "out the window"?
One might think so. But this "Power"...
when called upon, it calms my soul.

Yes...that's what I want to trust!
Something that gives relief. A source
that provides comfort. A substance
bigger than me...that dispels my anxiety.
Promising results may not occur quickly.
But they will come. Yes, that's what I
trust.

You say there are many of similar fashion
to trust. Yes. But I had to choose one...
as does everyone. And my choice is the
result of that "bond" I spoke of earlier.
That which has been "real" for me. Who then?
The "Three In One". The great "I Am".
So exceptionally trustworthy!

Looking For Words

Speechless. Stifled. Yet, not quiet paralyzed.
What is it that causes this emotional downfall?
Depression...of course. What else did you expect?

Life's everyday situations make a big impact, causing
a lack of passion. A day of too much solitude is of
no help. Hereditary make-up lends itself to increase
the undesirable state.

So, there is pain. Not acute at this point.
Nonetheless, its' existence looms steadily.
A dull pain. Could be deeper...thankfully it's not.
Just enough to bring about a lethargic haze.

To start motion with regards to responsibilities...
carries drudgery and a heavy weight. Quiet a load to
climb uphill. And right now, uphill is the only
direction life offers. Yes, a gloomy picture.

What does one do to combat this unwanted affliction?
Breaking the intensity is possible by taking small steps.
But really the key is endurance. The knowledge that
you have "beat it" previously. Knowing "time" is a big
part of the solution. "This time" is no different.

Feeling the pain is a must to overcome. As difficult as it may seem, reaching out to normalcy can begin the process to regaining a semblance of hope. It can start with any positive routine. May sound too simplistic...but before it has worked.

So, as I've been "looking for words", I found an agenda to solving my present painful dilemma. And I must bide my time while I endure. It is a tried and true application. Yet, in the midst of feelings, I easily forget this answer to regaining control. But it always eventually "turns up".

All the reminders and memories of past success... regarding the hurt inside, is only possible by God's Grace. Forever grateful.

Do I Dare?

A complete opening. Thorough
to the utmost. No denying. I've
done it before. And it's time
to do it again. In a different light.
At a different stage. Aging and
processing has brought on the need.

I've told Him before. I stated my
being...which He already knew.
Did He get mad? Was He disappointed?
I really don't know. All along, conclusiveness
has been sought. But always just out of grasp.

Time. It's time for settlement. No more
loose ends in my belief system. At times
it was thought resolved...alas, there remained
a dark corner. A corner that was ignored.
Well, not ignored...but no decisions had to
be made. Thus, it was not at the forefront.

The dark corner harbors such fear.
Abandonment...is this what scares so intensely?
Actions taken would seem to have proven
that the question had been answered. But not
so. No, not deep, deep down. In the pit of
the soul. A light...looking for favorable light.

Finally taking a chance. A total chance.
What will happen? I don't know. Am I doing
the "right" thing? For it calls for change in
core beliefs that can be felt in every direction.
I want to be in one accord with my Maker.
This above all.

Some agree...or at least accept. Others show
disdain. But when all is said and done...
it is between me and God. No one can give
permission. Nothing said by another will
resolve the issue. I must be totally honest
with feelings and desires. I have to come
to terms that only I can reach.

Terrific fear. And add guilt to the equation.
I'm stating my case. Not to another human.
But to the Deity who created me. So, I'm
"taking the plunge". Do I dare? I must...
for sanity. But will His reaction cause more
insanity? Am I headed for a statistic? God
banish that thought!

Why so late? Other complications with which
had to be dealt. So, a small...but very essential
portion remained unsolved. It was lived.
But always a hesitation regarding His approval
loomed. Sometimes remorse. At other times
an ignoring of fact kept doubts at bay.

Now...Do I dare? Yes. It is the only way
to gain peace. At least that's what I hope
will be the result. I'm telling my God
that I know myself. And I want to feel
as if He accepts my entire life.

I know He loves me. And He knows I love Him.
I believe this with all my heart. So, I have to
have the courage to believe that the mutual
love is enough. Enough to bring about a
positive view of the life I have already given Him.

You who read my write...it may seem such a
life of ambivalence. Yes, it can be "back and forth"...
"up and down". But the search for truth as time
unfolds, guides my quest. And I can easily say...
it is a search steeped in honesty. So be it.

The Open Book

What is it about some people? What makes them want to share their feelings? Is it the possible thrill of "shock value" coming from other people? Are they seeking approval? Is it the relief of a cleansing of the soul? Do they get satisfaction of expressing their opinions in a "round about" way? Are they looking for an answer? Do they want to be the center of attention? Maybe all these questions hold some of the reasons. One thing for sure...we are all unique individuals. But is it a type of weakness to share ones' inner self? Is it healthy? Surely, no one wants to become the target of ridicule and embarrassment. Given that statement, perhaps some people aren't as afraid or sensitive to judgments made by others. If no one else is apt to be negatively affected by the exposure of such thoughts, what's the harm? As for me, being an "open book" brings enjoyment. How so? I can connect with others, show genuine interest in people, maybe help someone else with similar emotions, be a guide for my own life, help conquer my fears, bring about needed change, maybe make someone laugh or smile. The list can go on. Isn't enough said? These positive effects are priceless. Simply, it just feels good! So, I'll continue to share and reap the benefits.

Religious Affair

Urged by fanatical spirits to have no worth.
In an environment where lights are dimmed to one
path.

Each choice provoked to decision.

Acceptance denied by vibes; surrounded by a
fabrication of beauty, peace and safety.

SJB April 24, 1991

Sunday 11:45 a.m.
(My youthful, more cynical years.)

Perspiration breaks from his forehead.

His voice, though centered, sounds from every
direction.

The three-pieced suit follows, as his body language
begins.

The pounding of his fist is magnified by the clatter
of watch and wedding band. People smile and gasp,
with awe and fear. Surely, he has been called.

SJB April 24, 1991

All The Children Of The World

"Confirmed" they say. And it must be done.

"Saved" they say. You must be won.

The deaf hear and the blind see.

At the name of Jesus, we all believe.

SJB 1993

Nets

There never is a time we don't need someone to lean
on.
And there never is a time we should push away a true
friend just to prove a point.
Each has place, space and time.

But let it be known, you will stand alone.
Wait...you are standing alone.
After seconds your knees give and you plummet into
the safety net,
held by those who made you stand by yourself.

As time goes on, the fall isn't as far.
You can judge how you'll land.
How amazing...the fear turns into excitement!

After an unusually good landing, you are getting back
on your feet.
And there stands a new significant other.

Oddly enough, your response is not to keep them
from the great fall.
But rather, take them to the top...above your friend
the net.

Because that now is your world.
Plenty of space to play and work.
Plenty of space to fall.

SJB 1992

Living In Truth?

Some think a simple answer.
Just do it! It's not that complicated.
Don't think about it.
In many circumstances it will resolve.

But not the case. Oh...they say too
much is made of it. Yes, in some
instances that has been the case.
What about the here and now?
Is it different?

The problem. In finding the solution,
is one living in a lie? Because others
do not understand, does that negate validity?
Confronted...one chooses not to argue.
But the words do cause "a rise".

Why can't there be solidity in actions?
Why does one linger about lost in
mind? Surely, one can take suggestions
evolving from care and concern. Is the
problem based on selfishness and carelessness?

What do you think? What do you do? What if
you're the one with the issue? Not feeling
understood, frustration sets in. It is not simplistic
to your person. You are hurting. Options tried
with no positive result. And yet others see the way?

Have those others been down your path?
Does their mind "click" like yours?
Would you fix the problem if you could?
Of Course! Why live in limitless pain?
Is it that you seek undue attention? Good
question. But why the endless suffering...
on purpose? You know deep down "no".

You are not expecting others to solve.
Can't they "get it"? Right now there is
no answer. You tell them so. And
yet with a different mind-set they try.
You are grateful they care.

Conflict arises. So needless...
yet inevitable. Why? Because you
are human...and so are they. Everyone
wants what is best. By the way, why
confide in the first place? Because
they are important people to you.

Does the fact that your thoughts
make no sense mean your trouble is
intentionally self-inflicted? Not in
your eyes, heart, soul and mind.
You don't want this painful albatross.

So, you must look to the next day...
knowing you will not gain their
understanding. It is not possible.
They are not you...and you are not
them. But it is ok. It's all part of
life. Your life and their lives.

And that's where it ends. We are all
different. Created uniquely by a Being
who knows what is best for all. And
hopefully that Being will soon bring
resolution to your dilemma. And
thanksgiving will ensue for all.

Abandoned

What? Family...solid and all around.
Friends...always there when it counts.
God...his promises are sure.
Society...are their standards applicable?
But what about you? What have you done?

So, with family...you avoid adult conversation.
You interact with the young...there it's safe.
Friends...you've taken a much different path.
Relating a minimum...but not intended.
God...your identity doesn't "fit" or so it seems.
Society...judgments, expectations impossible to meet.
You...you condemn and ostracize yourself.

Family, friends, God, society, you...not to blame.
Faults of sorts...but it is what it is. What then?
Where to seek console? An inner understanding
necessary for positive growth. Yes, you must delve.
Don't hold back. Seek affirmation within yourself.

True. You've been abandoned by your life.
Alone...fear...insecurity. But it's the only identity
you know. It doesn't jive with what's
known to be. Look again at family, friends,
God and society. There has been a perceived
harshness. Sometimes real. Sometimes imagined.
Separation and agony most definitely.

Now, it's up to you to accept yourself.
You must face reality. Possibly change beliefs
that have influenced your being. Are you sure to
take such a bold step? You have to...for happiness.
You must for survival. Throw away all? By no means!

There is hope. It may not be the usual.
But you have to resolve the fierce abandonment.
For the hollowness felt can no longer exist.
What's to be? You will find your way.

The most important step...know God is for you.
It will take prayer for guidance and faith in
His love. And by His love, you will begin to
love yourself. Hope, happiness and self-respect
will be sure to follow. Assuring desired safety.
How utterly appealing. Yes, the quest!

My Mother

When entering her room, she may be singing, in a chanting manner...her own "made-up" songs of praise to her Lord. Her clothing is usually disheveled. It is impossible to keep up physical appearances. Yet, her beauty continues to glow.

Most of the time her disposition is pleasant. There was a period of resistance at first. But soon her true nature returned. It seems at times her humor is intentional and other times it is just "out there". It causes much relief from tension. We have truly been blessed.

She hardly ever "brings up" her own children and grandchildren in conversation, without being prompted. She still remembers her son and oldest daughter, who both reside at far distances. But is often confused about where they live and what they do in life.

She remembers me, because I see her so often. But she often thinks I'm still in school and asks where I'm going to sleep at night. I'll answer her and a minute later she might ask the same questions.

She is still in love with her husband, who visits and eats with her every day. And he is still in love with her, but is lost without her. Their love for each other is so vibrantly evident. Their relationship is truly ordained by God. As it always has been...going on 60 years.

Although at this point in her life she is totally dependent on others...she commands respect from all who have been in her life. She doesn't ask for that acknowledgement. We just innately give it to her, because deep down she is the person we always knew. Regardless of the situation in which she is now trapped.

My Mother deserves every accolade that comes her way. She has always been a blessing to her family and friends. Her faith gave me sustenance when I had none. As a child, my fondest memory is when I laid my head on her stomach as she read to me. Her physical warmth gave me so much security.

My God gave me a precious, priceless gift in my Mother. And she would want me to give him all the praise. Tonight that is what I do, ceaselessly. Thank You Heavenly Father!

Defying An Answer To Prayer

We finally hand over the problem completely to our God. We have held on so tightly for so long. We analyzed, "figured", "talked it out", put our words in type, prayed half-heartedly and had very, very poor results. Now for some reason we are ready to "let go". And we do "let go"! There is a bit of peace that occurs and we are very grateful. Life is somewhat lighter considering the short amount of time that has transpired. Why, it has only been a few hours since we first sincerely asked God to take over the problem. He is doing just that. We are indeed thankful and find it hard to believe how fast prayer can work. Besides our prayer, we have asked others to pray for us. These prayers are being answered. It is marvelous. Then God makes the next move...a part of our request. But wait! We are not ready to "give in". He is continuing to fulfill our need and we are resisting. We know better than try to outwit God. So we kinda "draw a blank", trying to avoid our conscience. But it doesn't work. We can't stop thinking how we are "passing up" our chance of more answered prayer. No, we are not just "passing up" the help, we are defying our Maker's gift. Due to guilt, we cannot enjoy ourselves. But we continue on doing things our way. We have taken back what we had handed over. We are so stubborn and hard-headed. Lying to ourselves is not possible. We are somewhat miserable. Half of the prayer was answered and God is trying to answer the rest. And we won't let him. We will live with poor results again...By Choice!! Doesn't that "beat all"? What about that first part of the prayer He answered? Will He "cut that off"? Oh... we hope not! It was a miracle. And when we are ready for the second half of the prayer to be answered...will it come to past? We are really jeopardizing our future... as we continue to defy. We can't help but think that He is keeping a tally. Or maybe that's just the way we as humans would handle the disrespect, if we were in His shoes? We don't even think about asking for forgiveness...for we are still in the throw of our actions. This writing will end here because there is nothing else to be said.

Mind...Hear My Soul

How my soul cries out for mercy.
It is nothing that I have done wrong.
Rather, an amplified call for change.
This change...maybe a cure...
regardless, a different approach to life.

Like a slave, bound to the "ticking"
in my head. What a cruel member
of my body my mind can be. No, not
all the time. But too much energy has
been afforded this thoughtless, thinking
process.

Am I rational? By all means...yes.
That is the entrapment. I have notions
which are logical and progressive.
Yet this organ called the brain, also
allows lodging for less than sane
preoccupations.

Is my breath endangered? No.
But do I want to dwell in a coat that
is too thin for the elements? Not if
my will has any say so. So, it's up
to will power? Basically...yes.

And where do I go to "shore up" this
needed strength? Again...to my God.
Yes, He's been to my aid many times.
And tonight He's ready and waiting...
as I stand in His presence unveiled.

Why doesn't the soul have physical
matter? Maybe if it did my mind would
take more heed to its' interest. But it
doesn't. Even more reason to assure
my being to my Maker. For He knows
hour and purpose.

Will power required? Praying to have
an ample supply. My God says He
will give if asked. I believe this to be
true. Why? Because He has "come
through" time and again. He has
already worked miracles in my life.

Miracles...what? Yes, regardless of
this evening's surge of despair, I can
count numerous blessings. Happiness,
contentment and peace. I hear you say...
You must be joking...after all the prior
wailing? Truly, the gifts He has given me
are bedded deep down...where? Why,
how about that...they're bedded in my soul.

So, tonight I retreat from the battle I'm
trying to win. There are now only hints
of apprehension. I've voiced what I need
and my Master heard the sounds. He
brought to the fore front that He has been
my refuge before, and He's here again.

I feel confident that my mind and soul will
be friends once more. They seem to have
stopped their fighting for the time being.
And I'll "jump on that". I pray on waking
the cessation will continue. I hope for
the morrow to hold a blend of the treasures
already acquired. It is possible. With
Him all things are possible. God HAS
had mercy on my soul. Much Praise!

And Yet...There Are Good Memories

As I sit here at my computer, I'm listening to the "Grease" and "Mamma Mia" soundtracks. They are some of my summertime music. I tend to be seasonal with a lot of my music selection. Of course, I have my truly favorite artists whom I listen to year round. I guess I was in about 9th grade when "Grease" was released. I remember one afternoon a bunch of us girls piled in my friends' Ford Maverick...a tight squeeze... and headed to the movie theatre. It was an old theatre in an older part of town. I think we paid a dollar to get in to see the show. And the quality of the film was worth about 50 cents! Skips and scratches throughout the screening. Of course, the movie/musical was great. But I also remember having tempered panic attacks. And felt somewhat trapped in the theatre, even though there were only a handful of people viewing the movie. I was more than ready to go when it was over. At that point in my life, how was I to know of my severe mental illnesses? It was just the way it had always been. I didn't know I could feel any different. So, that's the way I functioned for the first 20 years of my life. Depression, obsessive-compulsive behaviors and high anxiety...all throttled by extreme irrational fear. One might think that given my situation, I would not have any good memories. Not so. I had fun times and have some enjoyable recollections. For instance, "wrapping" a friends' house...you know, covering it with toilet paper. It was late night, after a high school football game. We used 27 rolls of toilet paper! Great fun. Then there was the church youth trip, in which the guys and girls pulled pranks on each other. We girls had really given the guys a hard time. In return, they put itching powder on our toilet seats and in our sleeping bags! That was pretty rough! We deserved every bit of it. Of course, there was cruising up and down "the drag", especially on the weekends. Hanging out at Taco Bell and Pizza Inn. Driving late at night on a very remote Deep East Texas road, to see "The Lights of Saratoga". Fading lights that appeared down the road...probably from natural gases. But of course, a headless railroad worker swinging a lantern was the story line. Naturally, we didn't really believe the yarn...but the whole escapade proved to be some scary fun. Even though I would be having fun, my mind, at the same time might be in torment. The intensity of my illnesses was so potent that I could very easily and justifiably look back at those years and label them "all bad". And for a while, right after I started getting relief from medication and psychotherapy, I did see my past as all black. But through the years, I've been able to pull the good out of the bad with regards to my health as a youth. That truly is claiming power over my disabilities. I'm not giving up the fond memories to that destructive thinking of the past. At the same time, I'm not "painting everything rosy". No...I was in a living hell. And that's an understatement. All the while, coming across as sane as any other child or teenager. During my "growing up" years, mental health awareness was still in an infant stage.

Thankfully, much progress has been made to deal with such impairments. So, my friends who are parents and grandparents, take heed to possible symptoms that may be apparent in your youth...using your sight, hearing and gut feelings. It is never too late. And shame should not be anywhere in the picture. Make sure you give your children the chance to have some good memories. It's not the material, it's the mental. God Bless.

Wishing For More

The day began early. There was necessary communication for the planned daily actions.

Midday lent itself to spending mealtime with a dear friend. Talk was light and free. Good vibes, regardless that it took place in an institution.

Interaction with family was special. Despite "hard to face" situations, the closeness and conversation was positive.

During the afternoon, a best friend unexpectedly "dropped by" for a short visit. Since contact has been slim, talk was grand.

In early evening there was a scheduled gathering. Particular cause brought topics to the table. There was definite comradery.

Later, one brief phone call. And
two calls unanswered.
There will be no more contact until
tomorrow. Silence can be gold. But
it can also pain the soul longing for
more human aura.

Living alone...it is beloved.
No other habitat desired.
But at times it can hurt.

Happiness, Contentment and Peace...Oh Really?

Three valuable attainments.
Happiness...but you're not smiling.
Contentment...but you're restless.
Peace...but you have battles within.
You gotta be kidding me. Not you.

You've just spent two weeks in a
mental hospital. You must be depressed.
Happy...you can't be. You're saying
you can feel deep pain and fear...while
happiness resides?

You're still trying to find your place in
life. A searching is common to your
being. If this is so, how can you truly
be content? You're making no sense.

A war with frequent engagements takes
place in your mind. Confusion, desperation
along with poor judgment abound.
But you say you feel a peace in your
heart and soul? I don't believe you.

If you've acquired such gifts, how come
you're miserable so often? You are
making bold, conflicting statements.
Your problems and issues are rather
drastic. Yes, you lie to yourself.

Ok...tell me how you can be this person
you say you are. What? These traits
are settled in your core being? You say
they don't surface much? At least, not
right now. Why can't you control your
suffering if you possess these qualities?

Besides, you so lack self-esteem. Questioning
decisions, uncertainty is obvious. Derailment
of everyday life happens over and over. Always
having to start from scratch. You're not a good
example of stability.

Can you give me one good reason why I should
believe your professions? Bet you can't.
What? You say being happy, content and at
peace are the result of faith and hard work?

So, how did you ever learn how to achieve
what would be your potentials? I still don't
believe your nonsense. Wait...you say they
started small and have grown?

Now, you're gonna "throw in" the spiritual.
Figures...more nonsense! Alright, let me
hear more. You say your God lives in you?
If this is so, why do you seem so weak at
times?

It's spirituality? But you have many doubts.
Stop the cover-up! Get real! What? That's
it? Happy, contentment and peace comes from
faith? Oh...so you are saying these things
are not based on what happens to you. What
then?

Promises...they are promises. Your Maker
sees fit that even though you go through many
trials...types of rewards await? Well, that
sounds appealing. You are waiting to really
live instead of just survive? I hope you don't
have to wait too long.

You say a spirit fills you? And if you can't
ask for help...others are asking on your behalf?
Sounds like a "good deal" to me. I want that.
Yes, I want happiness, contentment and peace.
I'll follow your lead. You say "turn over"
my life to God? Kinda scary. Doubts flee!!
Get out of here!!!

Time. You say it takes time for these favors
to be revealed and "take root"? And I must
work towards them? I think I'll begin. If it
can "happen" to you...why not me? Indeed,
it's for all...so you say. God have mercy on
me and make Your truth come alive in my
simple, yet complex human being.

You say it's not perfection to seek? That's a relief. But steadfastness is the key. Honor and praise must be expressed with sincerity. And then let happiness, contentment and peace evolve amidst conflict. Thank you for "showing me the way". I'll pass it on.

A Forgotten Truth

They can bring together, but more often break apart.
Some are expressed too readily, while others just need
to be heard. We all have them..."opinions".

Opinions are needed to formulate action, bring about
change or keep things the same.
They can be harmful when used to prove an
intelligence, importance or virtue that exceeds others.

Let opinions be expressed.
But remember a few words that can eliminate
divisions, salvage family dinners and protect
friendships...

"I don't know. I don't have the answer...yet."

SJB April 30, 1991

OCD Partner

Ok...so you all know I'm OCD. Well, I've been obsessing about a "good thing" about to happen. Regardless that it's a good thing, obsessing can still bring intense insecurity and riddle one with fear...in a continual fashion. The other night, my sister called from overseas. I told her of my irrational fears. She suggested prayer. She said "Praying is much better than worrying." Simple right? I'd already tried to pray about it, but my boggled mind prevented much conversation with God. But at the time she suggested prayer, my complex mind "let in" an idea. I realized I would be expending a lot of energy both by praying or worrying. I knew I wasn't gonna be able to keep from obsessing. So, I thought...Why not obsess with God? We could both obsess about my unfounded fears together. That would be much better than being scared all alone. And so I began to let God obsess with me. Funny thing...Soon after this process began, my fears slowly began to dissipate! What a release. Now... knowing me, I'm sure God and I will obsess about this "good thing" some more. But I know I won't be alone inside my muddled mind. "What a friend we have in Jesus."

No Words...Or So I Thought

The high-tech piece of writing tablet is blurred.

There is no energy to express the reason for the dullness.

The situations, events and maladies which are the precursors to this state of being need to be conveyed. But where to begin? Will the truthful logic only stagnate while lethargy prevails? There are indications that aching is the next phase. Why so pessimistic? Because it has always been the routine. So, one must prepare for the worse. Not to fulfill a prophecy of plight. No... But to activate the survival mode. The only way to overcome.

Somehow, an explanation to appropriate parties who just arrived to the dismal scene is a must. Trusting that enough knowledge of the facts will transpire. With hopes that these persons will bring estimable relief... even if temporary. Yes, a bit of break in the cycle can instigate confidence that this circumstance will not last forever. Indeed, human connections are necessary to defeat the lurking madness. The past has proven that "reaching out" is a beginning. Others prayerful intercession to a God who seems at a distance is needed. You know God has not moved. But this overwhelming lot diminishes what spirit is left. How long will this dreadful existence last? Maybe days, weeks, or a month. No one is privy to such information. The hopeful prospect that the needed medicinal change will bring about promise, serves as a push for forward movement. There are inspirational sayings for such dilemmas. As for me, there is only one that brings about a sustaining "treading water" effect.

That saying: "Dig Down Deep".

My Dad...still here.

Tonight I struggled. A fight
within. A fear rising with thought.
Where to go? What to do?

He's 87 years old. He forgets.
His physical being is declining
in health. We argue. We agree.

The most important person in my life.
I have been afforded meaningful interaction.
He has always loved and accepted.
A stability he has forever provided.

Tonight I struggled. I needed to express.
And he was there. Listening. Stating
beliefs and admitting lack of knowledge.
He was there. He didn't dismiss.

So fortunate am I to be of his blood.
Long ago teachings, holding true in my life.
His way of living always making impression...
to this very day. And wisdom.

He is scared. He is experiencing loss of
great magnitude. At times very confused
by what his world has become. He's no
longer sure of his future.

Tonight I struggled. I went to him
searching for safety. And once more he
provided. He did this gladly...even in
his pain. And he told me to come back
when I needed.

Blessings shed. He has lived a life of
faith. He is strong even though frailty
pursues him. Yes, one day it will catch
up with him. But not at this moment.

"Daddy"...that's what I call him.
And he answers readily...as in the past.
Tomorrow we may fight and disagree.
I may "put my foot down". He may revolt.

Tonight I struggled. And he was there.
I told him "Thank you, I love you."
So grateful I had the opportunity to
speak those words.

I am an adult. He is elderly.
And yet...
I am still his child. And he is still
my father. A breathing treasure.
Much Thanksgiving!

"Modern Day Snake Pit"

Dysfunctional people in crisis, jam packed in a small facility. Shortage of workers. Half the staff seemed indifferent to the patients and the causes.

No psychological depth to any of the therapeutic activities. One group session consisted of the patients sitting in a room with the therapists just looking at them. No talking.

A type of reinforcement was directed at some patients, instead of trying to diffuse the inappropriate behaviors.

The hospital building was modern. Yet the methods of treatment were techniques of days long ago.

On the acute wing, it might be days before a patient was allowed to go outside to the fenced-in recreation yard.

Small seclusion rooms with a rubber mattress and camera on the ceiling were there for patients who "acted-out". And when locked in the room, the patient was stripped of all clothing and given a sheet with which to cover their body.

If a patient really "threw a fit" in anger, there was a stretcher/table to which they would be strapped down in "four points"....arms and legs spread apart. Again, a sheet was used to cover a body that was only wearing underwear. If the patient didn't settle down, they were threatened with a shot of heavy sedative.

An evasive threat was made by a nurse. Warning that the patient would not be able to see their family, if what that nurse considered unacceptable behavior continued. The patient was not sure who was "on their side". Were their parents in on this treatment?

Needless to say, no mental improvement occurred for the patient. It was a 6 month hospitalization. A type of institutionalization was beginning to form. Fortunately, the patient's insurance ran out, and they were discharged.

Why did this patient stay so long in a place producing such detriment to their health? Because they were depressed and didn't know anything else to do. They were at a loss.

This hospitalization did not occur in the "Dark Ages".
No, it was during the years of 1987-1988. Located in a well-known city in the States.

The patient found out in the following years that the "Modern Day Snake Pit" had been closed a year after the time spent at the hospital. It was "shut down". A result of insurance fraud. Figures. Says it all.

How does this writer have the knowledge and the "right" to tell these examples of such a hellish place? Because she experienced all of the above. Leaving nothing out. But "her will" saw her through.

"For He will give His angels charge over you."
Psalm 91:11

Title Fight, or so...

Swinging fists. Cuts, bruises
and swelling. Sweating, out of
breath. It is a "small-time"
match in a big civilization.

On the ropes, swaggering, falling
down. Head hitting the canvas.
Opponent's bare knuckles are felt...
even though gloved.

End of round. Stool to sit. Wet
sponges, razor cuts, spit bucket.
Emotionally "primed-up"...and
back out for more.

How many trips to the corner
will be made? When will the end
come? The crowd yells, cheers
for each punch that makes contact.

Body lands for the final time at
center ring. Winner? No.
Money made? Some. Will
your name be known tomorrow?
Probably not. The pain is just
beginning. It will take stolen time
for recuperation.

What makes you do it? A number
of reasons only a contestant would
understand. It is for sport. You
will be back if you're lucky...in
your eyes.

Are you a madman? Does it really
make sense? Is it fun? Is it worth
all the workouts? These fair questions
are asked. But they don't have to be
answered.

Let him be. It is his choice. None
of my business. Looking inward,
I see my battles. Are they for just
cause? Are they rational? Do I
"set myself up" again and again?

I am him. Yet there is absolutely
no chance of fame, money or glory.
The matches I bring on myself are
insidious. My training consist of
self-degradation.

Instead of climbing into a ring,
I wallow in my mind. It is not
a contest. But I compete against
myself. I can never be the winner
in my bouts.

So, I ask myself... Why do I continue
to be my own adversary? Is it that
I've grown accustomed to pain? Do
I just assume myself a loser? Is it the
only way to present myself to my person?
These questions I do have to answer.

It is time to retire from the profession.
I have no medals to show. But experience
to grow forward can be mine. That is, if
I apply what I have learned. Like the
prizefighter, it will be hard to give up
what has been for so long.

I want to begin this "after-journey".
It would be a new "card" for life. I would
start as an "opener". That meaning my
skills would have to be honed. If fortunate,
my perseverance and newly gained
knowledge could lead me to the "Gold".
God be with me.

The Sophomore

Laughter filled the locker room.
Her dress, although a year old, was still in style.
For some reason her perm was a bit frizzy.
It wasn't unusual for a tenth grader to have not had
an official date. Only God knows she reads her Bible
every night.

The laughter moved to the hallways, as the girls left
for their next class. Painfully, she realized everything
was all wrong. They were laughing at her. But they
weren't. They were laughing at the boy she sat next to
in algebra.

He didn't quiet fit in, and wore outdated clothes.
And his hairstyle was somewhat boyish.
Everyone knew he was turned down for
homecoming.
He hung with the church youth group.

Her heart relaxed.
She straightened her stance.
And her laughter blended with theirs.

SJB 1993

Be Strong, Relax, Let Go

We are all faced with times which seem to overwhelm us. There is no way to claim victory over an issue at the drop of a hat. Struggling, contemplating, at times verbalizing, and definitely praying are some of the characteristics of dealing with the problem. As I sit and write, I am experiencing a battle...but I am winning the war. Looking at the situation, three methods of combat come to mind. First..."Be strong". I've proven, by the grace of God, that I possess the inner power to overcome what is dwindling down to simply a nuisance. Wow...sounds great to refer to it as a simple nuisance, since it has been a heavy albatross for so very long. Having strength...no, not easy. But definitely possible. Next..."Relax". "Rome wasn't built in a day." Don't fret that all is not at ease. It will come. I know for a fact this to be true. How? Because it has happened with other issues in my life. So, just lighten up. Praying for a more carefree mind, right now. And then..."Let Go". Yes, "Let Go and Let God". He will stop the carousel in the mind from spinning. In fact, He wants the whole "playground"! So, there it is God...all yours!

And God...Just Where Are You?

There always has been controversy concerning where God should be found. I am no scholar of my faith, but I believe the most important place God should be found...is in the home. Whether one lives alone or the household is large in number, there He should reside. Let me be honest and clear, in my home I definitely fall short of letting Him "call all the shots". And yet, He continues to show His love for me. Going back in time, to the home in which I was raised...He was there. As a family, we had no "official" Bible study. But Sunday School lessons were expected to be read, as my parents prepared lessons pertaining to the church classes they taught. Prayers were said before each meal. When my brother, sister and I were young, we said the same prayer over and over. We took turns and this was the content... "Thank you for the food, flowers and sunshine. Amen." Usually, we said it as rapidly as possible. For there was a desirable meal waiting. When things got a bit "out of hand", my dad would pray a grown up, mature prayer. My mother would "pick up the slack" when needed. When I was in about 5th grade, my mother began breakfast with a short daily reading from "Open Windows"...a devotional booklet provided by the Southern Baptist denomination. Oh...sometimes it was so dreaded by us children. Half the time I was still asleep. But somehow I "heard". I guess that was a "God Thing". There was no religious music played from our beloved stereo. But when she had the chance, my mother played hymns on the piano. And more than often her voice could be heard singing in praise while she worked. All this attention to the God of our choice was present inside our man-made house. A house that was truly a home. My parents made sure God was available. They didn't quote Bible verses. No, they treated us all as equals. They made us feel worthwhile and respected our views. My parents didn't put pressure on us to "fit in" with others or expect unreasonable success in our endeavors. But wait...our home was not perfect. We had our disagreements, fights, scolding and reprimands. Sometimes serious...sometimes "light". Even so, my parents were never unfair. Did my parents have faults? By all means. But they paled so, considering life in general. Now to the present. Today as I walked into my mothers' nursing home room, my parents were holding each other's hand. And they were praying. My mother, despite her dementia, spoke words of hope and rejoicing that clearly "made sense". And my dad, with his head bowed and eyes closed was obviously "in tune" with my mother. Feeling very moved, I left the room to let them continue alone. Does the faith they have nearing the end of their lifecycle come from last minute confessions? No, it started over 60 years ago...in their home. So, this has been my experience as to "where to find God". I have been extremely blessed and am so fortunate. All due to the dedication my parents had towards their Maker. And the love...it exceeds! Forever and forever grateful! What have I learned from my upbringing? Why, to share the gifts. And share them generously! And it all begins in my home.

Actions Paid For

A choice. The "ball in my court".
Freedom...a release from authority.
Consequences are inevitable.
Good or bad.

What will I do?
It depends on the day and time.
Sometimes I'm conservative...
sometimes risky.

Do I dwell on my actions?
I guess it depends on how
vital the outcome will be
on a particular day.

The importance of the choice
will dictate how often I
"play by the rules" or when
I "throw caution to the wind".

Maybe I'm very proud and
pleased with what I do.
Or maybe I feel like shit
inside and out.

Wisdom or foolishness.
I'm accountable, that's part
of my freedom. Pleasure
or pain will be the result.

Let it go. Let it be.
Live with the outcome.
I'm an adult. Reap the
benefits or pay the price.

Don't dwell too long on
regrets. But don't forget
them. For the effects...
good or bad, will aid in
determining future choices.

Lord...Have Mercy!

"Lord...Have Mercy!" or "Lordy-Mercy!" I've said this a lot, mostly in a shallow sense. Not really turning the issue at hand over to God. Usually, out of exasperation...not expecting relief. Rather putting into desperate words a situation that seems unjust. And interestingly, I'm usually not terribly angry at that point. Because when I'm very mad I don't want my Lord to hear me. At least until I've cooled down and I can have a dialogue which doesn't include "color". But what about "mercy"? It is kindness and compassion towards someone who doesn't necessarily deserve it. Could be someone who is granted tenderness or forgiveness by a person with more authority. At least, that's my interpretation of the word. As I've already stated, in the past I've mainly used the term..."Lord... Have Mercy!" rather loosely. But the past few months, due to situations, I've reached deep inwardly and pleaded for help with these words. I did not feel as much easement as I desired. But I made it through to another day. And I did feel the presence of my Lord, on whom I had called. Considering my God and mercy, the following has been my experience. As a child I was taught the beliefs of the Bible. I witnessed my parents living the Christian life every day. When I was 10 years old, I basically said "Lord...have mercy!" But actually the words in my mind and heart directed to God were simply..."Here I am." At that moment, I felt a relief. Also, I remember thinking and saying to myself..."God IS real!" I was filled with wonderment at that realization. Such a good and true feeling. But life would continue with typical obstacles, and then some problems that were not so ordinary. Being an individual, even as a child, with obsessive thought processes...doubts and fears ran rampant concerning my spiritual encounter. Through the years, due to experiences, maturity, delving inward, medication, faith and prayers, much of the fear and uncertainty has been alleviated. When apprehensions arise concerning the authenticity of the experience with my God, I say in a very heartfelt manner..."Here is my belief. Help my unbelief." And then in a subtle way, the Lord has mercy on me. Granting some reassurance. Yes, I'm sure I'll say "Lord...Have Mercy!" in the future. Both when I'm merely frustrated as well as when deep pain occurs. And my God will show kindness, compassion, tenderness and forgiveness...as he has always promised. My gratitude will continue to be timeless.

Minds That Matter

You can do it! Anything is
possible. Think positive.
These words of encouragement
are said with care and best
intentions.

What if we've been trying?
We know that our God can
make all things possible.
We've tried to eliminate any
type of discouragement.
And yet the wanted change
has not occurred.

Put your mind to it. You
can do it! Again, said with
love and concern. We have
such supportive friends and
family.

Speaking of "putting our minds
to it"...therein lies the problem...
in our minds. Our minds don't
"click" like theirs. Ours are different.
We are all different.

For all of us, the mind holds our
deep will power. It is mechanical.
But everybody's gears are different.
Actions and reactions are not the
same. Timing varies.

We don't all have the same strengths
and weaknesses. We are truly blessed...
Our friends don't tell us... "Pull yourself
up by your bootstraps." For they know
us well enough to know our leather is
worn and perhaps torn.

So, what do we take from our loved
ones offerings? We take their belief
in us. They see something that we
cannot. It's powerful. And yes...
perhaps they overestimate our actual
strength to a degree. But that doesn't
matter...for they are there for us.

And what about our issue of which
we are dealing? In our "different mind"
we take what these people are saying
to us. And continue trying to apply it...
in a way we can relate to our being.
And maybe...just maybe, soon it will
happen. The desired outcome!

Then we praise Our Maker and
thank Our People.

Sharing

Sharing. Basically, we all know what it means.
Question is…Do we know how to do it?

With consideration to what we individually possess…
we each share something different. Makes for a
variety of gifts.

Are some things we share more important than other
allotments? I guess the recipient could give the best
answer…most of the time.

If at times we do not share, are we to be presumed
selfish? I don't think so. Some things are meant to be
ones' own.

And let's face it, some people don't want what we are
offering. Even if it's wrapped-up with a bow on top.
Keeps our ego in check.

I think giving of ourselves is the most important type
of sharing. Perhaps the hardest to render.

To share of self…What does this include?
I would think emotions, talents, hopes and desires.

Wait a minute. That's getting kinda uncomfortable.
That means we have to let someone "into our
territory".

Personally, I find it fairly natural and easy to share. BUT...I do have a few spaces that I "keep under lock and key".

So, I have to determine...Is holding back a necessary precaution? Or am I only hurting and cheating myself? Fear being the factor.

Ok...so I'm scared. As mentioned, some things are just for me. Except there are those areas, if I don't eventually share...I'll have regrets. And I don't want to leave this life with regrets.

The ball is in my court. I have the ability and common sense to know what and what not to share. Then, will I face my fears?

Yes, I believe I will eventually "slay my dragons". But it will be with prayer and on God's timetable.

Because it is my Maker whose guidance I'll seek... as I "take a leap" and learn to share completely.

The Elect...The Election

In another home with devotional ended…
politics and morals become the topic.

Outnumbered by the loudest few…
I'm learning that silence IS of gold.

My bumper sticker and vote say it for me.
A peaceful alternative.

SJB October 20, 1992

The Bumper Stuck

Blame You? I don't want to.
Blame Me? I don't deserve it.
Citizens For Appropriate Blame

SJB 1993

Grateful Release from Trauma

During the course of my life thus far, I have so many things of which to be thankful. I would like to share one of the most triumphant. I have experienced anxiety and panic attacks for all my days. Just in the past one and a half years they have greatly decreased. These horror producing sufferings started with a pure, almost constant stream of apprehension. I remember the first full-blown attack extremely well. I was in my 10th grade English class. We were taking turns reading aloud the book "Death Be Not Proud". It was my turn and I began reading. All the sudden, racing thoughts (a process of thinking which was not new to my psychological make-up) began to run rampant. Thoughts of wondering whether I had just said the "F. word" and other forbidden language drown my mind. My sight blurred. My body became cold and clammy. Then hot and sweaty. I wondered if I was in fact reading. Was I in a classroom or was my body elsewhere? Had I just reread and reread the lines before me? What were the words on the pages? The book began to shake. My voice quivered greatly, while I wondered whether I was really speaking. My heart was pounding "out of this world". I was very light-headed and breathing rapidly. Was I about to "pass out" and fall out of my chair? Was I fixing to "throw a fit"? Was I about to die? Finally, I had completed the paragraphs meant for me to read. Then came the thoughts...What had happened? Had I lost control? Had I made an extreme spectacle of myself? What were others thinking of me? With the conclusion of my reading, the symptoms slowly diminished. None too soon the bell rang, ending the class period. The only reason I could come up with regarding this utterly frightening experience, was that I was scared to read aloud in front of others. When I went home distressed, I told my Mother that I was scared to read out loud. I asked her to please not make me go to school again, until we had finished the reading of the book. Evidently my fear was so obviously great, it caused my Mother to call the teacher and ask her to not make me read aloud again. In fact, my Mother did not make me go to school the next day. Unheard of, in our family. This fear was to follow me all through the years. Sometimes the thought of losing control was great. Other times it was rather minute. But it was always haunting me. These uncontrollable thoughts began to carry over to other areas of my life. Sitting in church (especially in the choir loft when the youth choir sang), standing up in front of people, any gathering that was somewhat confined and indoors. It wasn't claustrophobia. Because it could even "slip-up" on me outdoors...in wide-open spaces. At that young age, I came to the conclusion that if I was really "saved" (a Christian), this insanity wouldn't occur. So, I suffered powerfully through many "invitations". When the evangelist would ask if there were any doubts in our hearts...I just sweated and questioned myself over and over. And of course, the result of the lack of true salvation would be a life waiting to enter into eternal hell. More fear. Through professional help,

I eventually learned about anxiety and panic attacks. Even with this knowledge, it did not keep me from losing consciousness for a period of seconds on one occasion. Oh people, there's so much more I could expound on regarding this hideous torment. I just want anyone out there who might be experiencing such despair...know you are not alone. It is not something of another world. You are not demon-possessed. You have done nothing wrong. It is a psychological ailment. It can be eased with medication prescribed by a competent physician, reputable psychotherapy and also for me...a positive 12-Step Program. Today, I have been released from the power this illness had over me. But, I am not letting myself think it will never happen again. That's too much of a chance it will surely come back to "bite me". I'm too scared it might not really be "whipped". So, I just praise God for the current relief and continue to ask for his mercy over the possibility of its return. At this point in my writing, I have nothing more to express but absolute, ceaseless gratitude. And that seems lacking. I hope I've helped someone today.

Words...Spoken and Heard

Words can bring positive communication and revelations.
They can also whittle away at self-worth.
So, there are good and bad words?
Not referring to acceptable utterance or profanity.

"Sticks and stones may break my bones, but words will never hurt me." Don't know about that. I've been hurt by words before. And I imagine you also have had bad experiences where words are concerned. Not that this fact indicates weakness on our part.

But let's look at the beneficial words. They can be spoken by family or strangers. The speech may be grammatically correct or just slang. If it comes from the heart, it can have the same impact.

How are we, as individuals, responsible for the effect words have on others? Does what we say really have that much consequence? Sometimes our words aren't heard...not necessarily intentionally. Other times, what we tell others "soaks in"...bringing much pleasure and joy to that person.

So, wouldn't it be for the betterment of society to share desirable expression? And each of us can do this. It is a matter of taking into consideration the welfare of the next person. Do we care if our statements make another feel either pain or delight? We better care! As humans, we are the only creatures who can explicitly converse in order to spread love.

Taking words to a higher realm, we look towards the sky. What does our Maker want to hear from us? Of course, He wants to hear of our faith and dedication. But what God really longs for is the sound of adoration drifting to His ears. Yes...that's it. The most powerful words spoken and heard, are praise to The Almighty King!

Banking On It

What is concrete in life? What is real? Who can truly be trusted? What or who can we "bank on"?

So much is abstract. We can't see it. We can't touch it. How can we come to believe in such things?

My supposition...it is necessary to base our faith on experiences that have already occurred. They do give us proof of what can be.

Personally, I bank on: my God's love, my parents' love, friends whom I can talk intimately, my dog's reliance on me, my church friends, my 12-Step Program and partners, the safety of my home, my beliefs, attitudes and values, my family and relatives, most of my choices...
I could go on. But I'll stop here.

All the things above that I can "bank on", have been tested and tried. They can stand on their own. And I can continue to reach back to the past and "touch" these objects. Even the ones that are impossible to see... have come through in grand thought and emotion.
And the things I've "banked on" have provided strength.

I think the key to "banking on" substantial things has to do with our choices. We do have minds of our own. Are we going to choose the materialistic world? Are we attracted only to people who have a certain amount of charisma...regardless of their intentions? Are we going to drift into a mind-set of unreality because it is easier with which to deal?

As I challenge myself for the future, I think my best bet is to continue to "bank on" what I have previously depended on in life. They have shown their true colors. It would be ignorant to chase after a reasonless rainbow, with hopes of finding Utopia.

So, now I'll step off "my soapbox". Cut through the wording. And commence to "bank on" the truths in my life. Friends...I do hope you find absolutes and relevance in your walk.
Many blessings.

Without Them

Life. It has been fragmented
and filled with illness. Some
poor choices and much upheaval
that could not be helped.

Am I to be mad at God?
Do I feel cheated? No...
There have been good times.

The conflicts so overwhelming.
Sometimes seeming cursed.
But not. No...Everyone has
their strife.

What has kept me afloat?
Two people. Partners who
gave me life.

They provided safety, security,
and stability. The couple
accepted me throughout extremely
adverse conditions.

Without them...no spiritual gifts.
Without them...no positive advice.
Without them...no inclusiveness.
Without them...no love.

Without them...my parents...
My name would be carved in stone.
A stone that would be a marker.
A marker telling a beginning and end.
A grave too soon covered with earth.

What Was God Thinking?

How can one be happy and content at their core, yet be suffering from maladies that cause such emotional and mental upheaval? It is strange...that is..."the mind". Pardon me if this is offensive to you, but... "Just what was God thinking?" Personally, I have no doubt that he has everything under control, even if we are spinning out of control. I mean there can be "a peace" within, but all the while everything is in turmoil. And it is a grand scheme...our bodies, the universe. The soul can be safe and sound, and at the same time fear persist. I am so grateful for the happiness, contentment and peace that has grown within me. But confused and exhausted from trials. Well, wait a minute, how did those qualities...happiness, contentment and peace develop in the first place? In retrospect, it's probable that they came to fruition by way of suffering, helplessness, loss, faltering and fright. And who did I finally turn to when the answer seemed hopeless? Why, it was God himself. Even if I was too overwhelmed to communicate effectively with him at the time, others were interceding on my behalf. So have I been too hasty to question God's plan for my life? I think not. He expects us to wonder why hardships come our way. If not, he wouldn't have told us to not worry in the first place. His whole being is reassurance. And of what do we have to be reassured? Of course...it is that we will overcome our strife. It all seems so complicated and insane...the whole basis of our relationship with our Maker. But there is an aspect of the connection between us and him that we must take into thorough consideration. That is his love for each of us individually. Love, the greatest gift. Whether it pertains to his spirit within us, interactions with other humans, or respect for all his living creations. Love flows through us as a feeling. What ecstasy we feel. And aren't feelings also the way the mental and emotional upheaval that was spoke of earlier conveyed? To put it simply, we have to take the good with the bad. Not what we want to hear. But then comes the base of our faith in him. It is not necessarily how much faith we have in him. It is that we do have faith in him. Because sometimes we are going to be strong and other times weak. Faith that his plan for our life is much better than what we had in mind. So let us rest on his promises. Yes, I can be happy, content and at peace while I endure tribulations. And with this ironic twist, all that can be said is "To God Be The Glory".

On Being Bipolar...at this moment.

Years ago it was called "manic-depression".
I think that term was more self-explanatory.
Not that I'm out to change medical vocabulary.

I suppose that name of the diagnosis seemed to
convey the emotions involved more poignantly.
Having a base personality of the depressive mode...
I feel there is more understanding among others with
the usage of the "old term".

"Bipolar" became more popular during the 80's...
as far as I recall. It kinda became "the in thing". It
seems it was the diagnosis of quiet a few individuals.
Whether or not it was an appropriate label for that
person.

I do know for a fact, both terms apply to me.
And a heredity of the disorder preceded my person.
That fact makes it easier to guide my medical
treatment. Seeing how other relatives handle their
obstacles helps me to activate my formula for
endurance.

So, at this moment...how does the above information help me? Well, the dissection brings me back to the reality that I've been down this road before. Thus, providing encouragement. And I know that later today, help will come from professionals that will hopefully bring about stability. I am confident, regardless of how I feel at this moment.

How Does One Approach Tomorrow?

Not each day can be bright, nor even have a glimpse
of light. Yet personal growth can be expected
to be the result of endurance.

This day does not hold a feeling of hope. The body
is weary of the effects of inner turmoil. Considering
the reason for the low ebb, there is not a solution
in near sight. So, how does one approach tomorrow?

This inner turmoil of which is spoken, has its roots
in everyday problems that each generation faces.
There is also an issue of a disorder in which a
maudlin psyche arises.

Again, how does one approach tomorrow?
So much is out of the hands. It seems impossible
to find any positive resolve.

Maybe it's time to take a look at our definition of
positive resolve? Well, stating those two words, the
first notion is a sense of "feeling good". But who said
positive resolve was an immediate salve?

No, if something in our life is positive, it doesn't
necessarily mean we like the effects it brings. It
only signifies it is for our own good...which
might be in the future, not the here and now.
I know...kinda a "letdown".

What about the other half of the term...resolve?
A resolution. Now that's something that is
not a guaranteed "good thing". But not too quick...
it's not a sure "bad thing" either.

How about this for some consolation? Resolve
may start out negatively and eventually come to
be extremely desirable. Again, time plays its part.
And of course, work is necessary for such change.

Did I say "negatively" in the previous statement?
Why, yes. And the opposite of negative...positive.
That brings us back to original term of this
writing..."positive resolve". Maybe resolve occurs
before it becomes positive. More waiting!

So, we take resolve however it comes to us.
For sure, it brings a bit of peace...for the
situation to be sorta settled. At least for
the time being. Bottom line...work and wait.

Well, back to the question..."How does one
approach tomorrow?" Possibly, simply letting
go of the "hard-headed" belief that we are gonna
have "the answer" tomorrow, brings a realistic
view that is somewhat comforting.

And when one rests and processes the situation…
there comes a time for faith. Yes, a belief that
there will be a solution to our problem. Maybe
it's time to take our hands off of trying to "fix" things.
We've done our job with some success. But now
it's time to turn the issue over to our Higher Power.

This is where we place our problem. For me,
I now leave my issue at His feet. And see that
personal growth is beginning, as I've already
endured trying to "figure things out".

It is now the morrow. I do not have the answer.
But there seems to be a slight "air" of good
"positive resolve". A bit of peace resides within.
These results are far more than expected when
this writing began. Grateful.

Sensational

Some bodies can sense everything. Not only do they experience the basic emotions: mad, sad, glad and scared. But they encounter all the "pins and needles" that can come along with those feelings. And it can be a very intense physical sensation. Most of the time these extreme occurrences can bring peaks of fear. Very unpleasant...frightful. And it's all within the body. No one else can see what that person is trying to endure. These senses can be brought on by everyday situations or be the result of a person's basic body chemistry. They have been born with this disadvantage, which has been a part of their life all along. If the latter is the case, the individual has usually developed coping mechanisms. These skills don't necessarily "snuff out" the problem, but they can help a person "get by" one more time. And then there's always the "next time" to dread...again, dread with increased apprehension. These "pins and needles" can explode into panic and anxiety attacks. Absolutely terrifying and miserable. As someone who experiences these episodes, I've found that taking prescribed medication according to a physicians' orders is a big relief. And I am cautious, because an addiction can occur if not being in accord with my body. Taking the medication when it is necessary, after an attempt to "talk out" my anxiety. Either describing my plight to another person or just hashing-out the feeling within myself. Hoping that will curb the feeling, foregoing medication. I have often said..."I can feel a leaf move." Throughout my life, that was the circumstance. But I can thankfully say that these very uncomfortable states have lessened drastically, just in the past couple of years. I do not try to figure out the reason for the decline. I don't want to "go there", lest the intensity returns. I guess I don't want to "jinx" myself. May be silly...but I don't care. That's just where I'm letting this issue rest. And I know that God has allowed me to presently withstand and overcome. Tremendously grateful!

When "The Immediate Family" Is No Longer

Those who came before us are slowly vanishing.
What does this mean to those of us who are left?
It seems that we still have questions we need to ask.

Their advice, which nearing the end has
become somewhat distorted, is no longer accessible.
Yet their prior wise decisions, continue to keep their
authority in high esteem. Those memories are solid.

Where does a person, who relied on these people
for their immediate family go to "fit in"?
It's not that this individual has no friends or relatives.
But the sign of infinity has been fragmented and
broken.

Because of the departure of an older brother and sister
when this individual was younger, the parents and this
youth formed a family unit within the original family.
They experienced good times and hard times together.
A special bond.

This single adult who has no children to call family,
begins to reach to nearby cousins and close friends
to fill the void. Not to dismiss the siblings. Fact
is, they are at a very far geographical distance.

At times this empty space seems vast. Other times
the understanding and acceptance of the life cycle
override, and all is well. The blessing is that this
person has lived alone all her life. So there is no
dark vacancy in the living quarters.

The answer...continue to "reach out". Don't isolate
more than usual. Those cousins and close friends
will provide interaction and sense of family needed.
Fear will be present. Pain due to the loss of the
only immediate family ever known will be felt.

But again...reach out, search for new life. Be
"a part" even when you feel apart. At this point…
the individual must try new things. Ugh!
Oh...how it goes against the grain.

Yes, a different life is beginning. Tonight,
this person feels up to the challenge. She
won't always believe in progress with this
issue. But forward movement will eventually return.

Has someone been forgotten? Why...yes!
It is the all-knowing, always present Almighty.
This human had forgotten that she can rely on
"The Way, The Truth and The Life."
Yes, forming a new immediate family is possible.

For a Better Me, For a Better World

Must I take a stand? Need I hold a hand?
Does what I say cause others to take consideration?
These are traits of leaders and innovators.
Yet, the difference begins with me?

Buildings have their names. Statues remember their deeds. Offices held and money made. How vital their contributions and the differences they've created.

Standing on my own. Holding out my hand to give or receive. Speaking, even in fear...and listening to decipher. These are traits of leaders and innovators. And yes, the difference begins with me.

SJB 1992

Obstacles

Obstacles. One tries so hard to overcome. The endless searching for an answer to a plight which possesses a person. Perseverance, faith, hope...they all seem to be of no help. Such a gray picture is being painted. It is a trial. No one is immune to this misery. The overwhelming sensation can bring one to their knees. It can cause irrational actions and behavior not typical of the person involved. The slightest possibility to beat the dreaded difficulty must be the impetus to keep an individual on course. Or to put it more frankly...help "keep a person's head above water". What if someone has a solution to the problem, but that solution also becomes an obstacle? Such a predicament...truly. What causes us humans to resist an answer to a problem? Is it the fear of change? Could be. What makes rationality "go out the window"? Is it because prior rational actions taken have not solved the problem? A good chance. Honestly, who wants more failure? But one must keep trying to rid themselves of the fear that lack of success produces. Obstacles can bring about fierce torment. This picture is getting darker. But it is factual. Does an individual continue to call for help from their God? By all means. Because therein lies the elusive solution. Whether response from The Almighty comes sooner or later, one must hold onto the beliefs that are rooted in their soul. So, how to remain calm while waiting for an answer? Again, a cry to one's God is absolute. A shout out for mercy over and over may be required. So what good, if any can come from this bleak writing? For there has been no resolution. Maybe to let another know they are not alone in their thoughts. Yes, someone out there feels the same. In fact, this all-consuming dilemma may be common...if truth be known. So, for our comfort..."I waited patiently for the Lord's help; then he listened to me and heard my cry. He pulled me out of a dangerous pit, out of the deadly quicksand. He set me safely on a rock and made me secure. He taught me to sing a new song, a song of praise to our God..." Psalms 40:1-3.

"The Way We See Things"

"The Way We See Things" is really the way we believe and feel, according to our life thus far.

What if "The Way We See Things" is our physical ability to see things? Controlled by blindness, nearsighted, farsighted, and diseases of the eyes...our sight can be limited.

What if "The Way We See Things" is what we see? Wheelchairs, shoplifting, parades, various colors, car wrecks, beautiful sunsets, hidden bruises, funeral processions, smiles and food stamps.

"The Way We See Things" is the way we believe and feel. Look and see...and know that the beliefs and feelings of each human can become an attribute to you.

We can easily see differences on the outside; and invite or decline. But unexpectedly, some of the biggest differences occur on the inside. Friends and family can be foreign.

If we use our eyes to look and see. And hold a hand to believe and feel...

It can change "The Way We See Things".

SJB May 11, 1993

Cats and Dogs

Cats and dogs. What wonderful creatures. They can fill an "empty spot" in your heart, even when you didn't know there was a vacancy. When a cat or dog depends on a human for shelter, food, trips to the veterinarian and affection, it can complete that individuals' need to "take care" of something. I have never experienced trying to fill the needs of a child. And it's just been in the past two years that I've been "needed" by my parents. But through the years, I've almost always had a furry companion that required my attention. Living alone all my life, the bond that has developed with each of my pets, has been nothing short of kinship. And it's amazing how a pet can "take on" their masters' personality. It may not be mirror image but there is a reflection. For me and my "make-up", the 1990's held more mania than usual. During this time, I had a cat named Corky. Did I just mention that pets can take on their masters' personality? Well, let me tell you...poor Corky...she was bizarre! A bit psychotic... had to be. But one particular day, when I was on the downside of an episode, this God-given animal curled up beside me...not to leave my side. She knew I was in pain. And even though she was not a real affectionate cat, she let her guard down...just for me. The past ten years I've dealt more with obsessive-compulsive and acute anxiety disorders. (By the way people, I'm not trying to make more of these illnesses than the truth. I come by them honestly. I can look at relatives...you

know..."blood", and say..."Yes, this is the real deal.")
At any rate, ten years ago, I went to a farm barn
stall which was the birthplace to a litter of miniature
dachshunds. There I picked out my present apartment
mate. Lilly is her name. She has long, soft hair. But
she gets a "summer cut" a couple of times a year...so
she's also short-haired...for awhile. Getting back to
the psychiatric disorders mentioned. Unfortunately,
Lilly has placed a claim on the features of which she
has sensed and witnessed. She can be an alarmist. A
certain amount of panic is woven in her personality.
Really...a bit too much. At the sound quieter than a
pin dropping, her head and torso "fling up" from her
lying position. A bark usually ensues. When out of her
territory or comfort zone, she's at a loss. Not knowing
which way to run, fear fills her eyes. Her body can
be so physically rigid and tense at times. I must say I
have a certain amount of unwarranted guilt regarding
her symptoms. Nevertheless, when I come home and
unlock the door, she is there with her tail wagging,
leaping up and down. She's obsessed with her daily
schedule. This actually makes her easier to take care
of. She knows what I expect of her. And I know what
she expects of me. She wants me and I want her. She
knows she's mine and I know I'm hers. She relates well
to people. But if she thinks I'm leaving her in someone
else's care, there's a look of... "What are you doing?
Where are you going...without me?!" And it is a look
of fright. Regardless of the undesirable traits that
she's acquired, she knows all about love. Amidst all
the "clutter" of disorders, there is steadfast caring. At

night, she lays down on her bed...on the floor at the head of my bed. She is relaxed, calm and fears nothing. She knows I'm beside her. And I know if I need to be awakened with urgency...I'll hear her bark of warning. Oh...also, we talk aloud all the time. Because of this mysterious communication between human and animal, we know what each other is thinking. And we do have fun...even dance sometimes! Do I take the relationship with my dog too seriously? Maybe. But if you live by yourself...you understand completely.

Try and Understand

Mental disorders can readily affect your daily routine. You may look and sound perfectly reasonable. But inside, your brain can be in constant commotion. Fear, racing thoughts, and paranoia can reside within your head. How does one function on an everyday basis in the real world, when faced with such a dilemma? It is very hard. And what if people expect you to perform tasks which are not within your capabilities...just because everyone else seems to be able to "pull them off"? A feeling of guilt settles in your already disturbed mind, because you feel as if you aren't a dependable human. There's the guilt that you aren't contributing to society. And the pain. It is foremost. But no one else can visualize the scars it leaves. Wounds that reopen time and again. Many times you may attempt to explain your thought processes, but it seems as if it falls on deaf ears. Of course, there can be genuine lack of comprehension on the part of the average person. It is not their fault. But there continues to be expectations from others, of which you can't fulfill. What self-esteem you might have about yourself "goes out the window". Only to leave you feeling more unworthy. There is nowhere pleasant where you can retreat and regroup. People in the world are interacting with each other with relative ease...so it seems. Oh...they have their problems, but they have an ability to still function in a usual manner. Perhaps you sleep too much, making you feel as if you are just a lazy person...

irresponsible. Or you might not sleep at all, giving way to physical weariness. Unable to accomplish much the next day...again irresponsible. At least that's the picture painted. Possibly your personal grooming seems too overwhelming. You appear indigent. It is true, with mental illness it is possible that one continues to "shoot oneself in the foot" time and again. But it might not be able to be helped. Others might think you are merely setting yourself up for failure. Not really trying to change your predicament. Change...that seems entirely impossible. You are stuck. Keeping a home clean may be out of your reach. Socialization starts to fail. Eating healthy falls by the wayside. Isolation is preferable. The desire to get "out and about" diminishes. An inner anger builds...which erupts on occasion. Sometimes in the presence of bystanders. How humiliating. Reinforcing the idea that you don't belong in social settings. And then there's the lack of monetary gain, which causes limitations. When all the characteristics above hinder a person once or twice in their life, there can be a rebound with much success. But what if you are constantly battling these adversities on a regular basis over a lifetime? Maybe you still struggle to a degree with these "demons" while receiving proper medical care. This is when "flat-out" survival instinct kicks in. You have to find some compassion towards yourself... within yourself. You have to make a gratitude list. You have to find some way to be "easy" on yourself every once in awhile. You have to make your life as simple as possible. You have to find a small success among your failures. You have to call a friend, even though you don't want to. After two weeks of laying on your parents' sofa, you make it your goal for the day to drive around the block…to buy a coke at the convenience store. This is how you begin to function again. Keeping in mind, you'll probably have to use these strategies again in the future. So you learn to live in the moment. Enjoy pleasures as they come your way. Laugh at the least thing that is funny. Run an errand for an elderly "shut-in". Tell your family that you love them. Make a positive "little" matter "bigger". Listen for the strings in a moving song. Give a big cheer for your favorite sports team. Most of all, be grateful.

Spiritual Concept

Wanting to reach to you, and reaching to you collide in fear. Your love makes me stand back! What is your love, but your life? A life that helps me in my life. I believe you know what I feel inside.

For me, to know you is to grasp you in my mind and heart...and see you in others. Belief and acceptance; helping others; an occasional "spiritual high"...
(An acute awareness that you are real).

My goal - more communication with you.
All of this is what makes you real for me and in me.

SJB December 25, 1993

When Depths Return

How is it one works so hard to overcome…
and yet deterioration sets in and the albatross returns?
And this is after such huge success with regards to
dealing with the issue…or maybe if we clarify, it will
shed some light…we are dealing with a disorder not an
issue. The word disorder brings forth its' magnitude.

What an extremely hard, scary, day of agony when the
"demon" rears its' ugly head again. Haven't we had
all we can take? When does it end? That is it…there
will be no end. Not on this earth. Sometimes heaven is
beckoned to present itself. Although, that brings about
a fear of the unknown. Even so, that is where our mind
has settled.

We reach out for help. And it is there for us. But no
immediate relief is possible. Treading water at best.
The disorder is dealt with every day. It is always
a source of contention. We learn to live as normal
as possible. Of course, one questions if there is indeed
a "normal". At times we handle the disorder with a
great amount of ease. And other times it is torment.

So, what to do with this "abnormality"? Well, we continue to reach out for help. And we put our whole heart into following instructions given, that are provided to regain some type of hope. Even if we are skeptical. Pain, fear and numbness persist although we are taking steps forward.

We must claim endurance as our ally. We've fought this battle before, even if some of the characteristics are new to us. We "hear" people when they tell us that we are not alone. It is a time to do anything that will make us feel better...as long as it is not harmful in the end. And we let others pray for us. We wait. Surely light will return. Yes...it will.

Valentine's Day 2013

Several years ago, I was at a particularly low point. Even so, I had not reached horrific despair which would have refrained me from voicing a bit of sacrilege. During this pain, I told my mother..."Heaven better be good!" In her beauty, she replied..."Sara, I don't think anyone will enjoy heaven more than you." What an instinctive motherly thing to say! Helping restore my faith and self-worth. Making me feel like I was the most important person in God's eyes. And she said it "as a matter of fact". My pain did not immediately diminish, but her sustaining peace guided me to better days. Happy Valentine's Day to MY two sweethearts... Momma and Daddy! I have been richly blessed!

February 14, 2013

In The Middle Of It

There aren't many words.
The emotions have been dulled.
There is work in motion to overcome.
But it will take time for change.

Pain is beginning to evolve.
How much will it affect functioning?
Actually, day to day living has already been altered.
One cannot predict the severity of the impact to be
made.

Sleep once provided relief.
But because that source has recently been despised…
the usual formula for "getting by" is unsure.
There must be some bandage for waking hours.

The fact that there is a "remedy in the making"…
must provide the necessary anchor. That is the origin
of security. All the known powers that produce safety
must be called on. This is called "being in the midst" of
a powerful, dreaded force.

A Blow to a Hard Head

It may be looked at as constructive criticism. Or perhaps just plain embarrassment. Hopefully, it is a positive life changing experience. Actually, all these descriptions fit the interaction I'm about share. At the time, I was in my early 20's. I was in a psychiatric hospital for depression. I had been there for about a month. The hospital provided a very progressive program for their patients. It was called "ADAPT". I can't remember what the letters stood for...which doesn't matter at this point. It was my first psychiatric hospitalization. I never experienced another hospital program which produced such a dramatic change within myself. Unfortunate for the future of mental health, it was nearing the end of long-term psychiatric inpatient care. We had all kinds of therapy... group psychotherapy, music therapy, art therapy, occupational therapy, recreational therapy and more. My memory fails me. It was a long time ago! We patients had little "time off" from trying to "get our act together". At any rate, on weekdays we had three different group psychotherapy sessions. They lasted from 1 to 1-1/2 hours. And no one who attended, which was everyone on the unit, got away from being a "target" of the process. At first, I didn't say much at all. I wasn't going to "open up" like everyone else. I'd show them! But eventually, my barriers started breaking down and I began to talk. And I found that most of the time after I talked, I felt better. A lot of times more confused...but better. Of course, I "assumed" all the time. I was sure I knew what others thought of me after I talked. And usually, I assumed the worse. Like I said earlier, I had been there about a month. I was learning how "group" worked. The "opening up", the consolation from others, the confrontation from therapists and other patients, the denial, hopefully insights gained within...the possibility of the opportunity for change in behaviors and feelings. A "breaking down and building up" procedure for the better. I found everything about group to be interesting and to my liking. Seeing how other peoples' minds worked. I found myself giving input where others were concerned. A lot of times I was on target with my comments and analysis. Also, I was beginning to look inward. Yet it was very turbulent and perplexing. I was starting to "hear" what other patients and staff were telling me. So, I began to talk more. There was one nurse I liked in particular. And deep down, I wanted her attention and approval. Her name was Ellen. But it seemed at times when I would tell her something, I'd walk away frustrated at her retort. I didn't know then, because I was so blinded by my brain, but she was constantly confronting me. Breaking me down. Not in a "mean" way...just sharp and to the point. Her responses could make me start to "boil inside". On Wednesday's...right after lunch, we had the head psychiatrist, a nurse and a therapist all in the group session. Usually, "no punches were pulled". But a "building up" was to follow...if the patient allowed. So, I was beginning to see things within myself and it was kinda exciting. Well, one Wednesday, we gathered for this "main group" of the week. There were about 20 patients in the session. We were all seated and the doctor asked who wanted to "start off" the therapy. I was in a pretty good mood. Why not? I was gaining insights. So, when he asked who wanted to speak, I piped up and said about a sentence and a half. Then Ellen broke in and said..."Sara, be quiet. We've heard enough from you!" OH MAN...she just didn't!!! I sat there shocked. I was fuming inside and totally humiliated. I continued to sit there in that "state" for the whole hour and a half. When the group was over, I hit the door...the first out. I went to my room, not sure what my next move would be. Then I thought, I'll go outside, climb a tree and not come down until they come looking for me. Doesn't sound like someone in their early 20's. But my mind had been broken down to infancy. So, I went to the elevator to go downstairs and outside. I was the only person waiting for the elevator. While I stood there, Ellen came up to me. She had something in her hand. She stuck out a roll of Lifesavers. She said..."Candy?" I wasn't looking at her. I replied in an extremely mad but quiet voice..."Nope". She then asked..."Mad?" I said..."Yep." Then she had the gall to say..."But you stayed and listened". OH...was I furious. She was right again! I didn't respond in any way. I just stood there looking straight ahead at the elevator door. She then walked away. I was relieved I wasn't gonna be cooped up with her for three floors! So, I went outside and climbed that tree. I think I lasted for about 20-30 minutes, then came down. What was I thinking? Nobody was gonna come looking for me. But I sure wasn't gonna talk in group therapy again! Of course, I did. And it wasn't really too long after the confrontation. I was learning. And there was much, much more learning about myself and my mind to come from that hospitalization. I began to stop looking to Ellen for approval. But I "heard" everything she said. In fact, after the incident, I started "hearing" a lot...from everyone. Not that they directed it all to me. But I could see insights that applied to me, through each of their issues. I had such transformations within that 3 month hospital stay. My thinking process truly had a renovation. In fact, towards the end of my days there, I began to sense (whether or not it was true) that the staff kinda looked at me as some sort of "prized pupil". This only built my confidence and basically made me feel good. I saw that I had had an extraordinary overhaul of the mind. On the day I was discharged, Ellen pulled me aside to a vacant interviewing room. She told me how proud she was of me and my accomplishments. She said not many people had done what I'd done. Thing is, I did not have to hear that from her to secure my pride and belief in myself. But it was definitely "icing on the cake"...and it tasted great!! Years later, I "ran across" her in another area of my life. I was then able to thank her and tell her how much of an impact she had made on me. Because at that older age, I could say she was one of the most influential people in my life. And I had the privilege to tell her. I am so grateful that I was allowed to be a part of such a progressive psychiatric program. I am very, very fortunate. Not many people have been given that chance. Thank you, all the staff of Beaumont Neurological Hospital...Beaumont, Texas. The year of 1985.

He's Tired...He Hurts

Many years of consistency.
His body healthy...save a couple of scares.
His work purposeful and beneficial.
His children experience good and bad...life.
His faith always sure. Never afraid to question.
His "Love"...forever one unit.

What's happened?
His physical strength no longer "solid".
He seeks to perfect an occupational goal...when able.
His offspring continue with the "ups and downs"...
again, life.
His core beliefs intact. But the "unknown" is at hand...
apprehension. His "Love"...slowly disappearing...and
now, all but gone.

Presently.
He knows his body is only a "house".
His achievements have, and continue to help society.
His son and daughters are now his parents.
His "Power"...in his soul. Hopefully it guides,
consoles and gives confidence. His "Love"...he longs,
he pains. Slowly letting go...may be subconscious.

What to do?

I can see that he receives the best of care...regarding bodily health. I can laud and appreciate his accomplishments of work. Let him know. I can strive to be a worthwhile human and member of society. Make him proud. I can pray to my God. Prayers for his welfare. Grateful that he introduced me to the Deity. I can continue to love and care for his "Love". Recognize his ache and try to soothe.

The future.

The spirit in his body will be made anew.

The progress he made in his field will always be gain.

The kind of person I am...well, I want to resemble him.

The King is on His throne. The "Love" of his life... together again, they will experience new heights.

But for now...

He's tired. He hurts. He's my father. How he makes my pride grow!

Bipolar Odds and Ends

There are many facets to Bipolar Disorder. It is not just a manic high or depressive low. There are unexplainable quirks, bizarre thoughts, fears and characteristics which accompany this disorder. Just when you have one undesirable trait under control, another takes its' place. And of course, the same traits can reoccur at the "drop of a hat". A person may have the appropriate medicinal regimen for 2-3 years, then their body chemistry changes and they have to search for different medication that works for them individually. Many people nowadays have an idea of the highs and lows that exist. But living day in day out with the additional oddities is another story. They are nearly impossible to articulate, much less does one have the ability to help another person get some sort of grasp of what they are experiencing. A person who has Bipolar Disorder hopefully has doctors, nurses and therapists who understand and can treat these frightening and disturbing features. If not, that individual is in a hellish state. This disorder cannot be completely conquered. One has to learn to live with it... play by its rules. There has been much advancement in dealing with Bipolar Disorder. Thank God...truly. But a person severely affected does not know complete freedom from its curse, regardless of monumental positive progress. So, what of all this bleak talk? Let's just be kind to each other every day. Who knows what another seemingly healthy person may be encountering? All this said for "better living".

My Lord Told Me

My Lord told me to come to him when I am weary. Well, Lord...here I am. I'm tired, fatigued and exhausted. I'm "spent". The definition of weary in the dictionary goes further. It uses the terms crumble, break down and totter. It also says: make or grow impatient or dissatisfied with something or at having too much of something. Specifying, it can be physically or mentally. Man, that's "quiet a load". At this point, I'm "zeroing in on" the part about being dissatisfied and having too much of something. I'm dissatisfied because I have no control over some actions of others, which directly affects the way I feel. It is not that I'm letting it get to me. That is too simple of a way to view the issues. These situations which are causing strife cannot be harnessed, at least at this point. I'm choosing the battles of which I do have control. And trying to let the rest just fall into place. Truly, I have no other choice of action. So, I'll let that be...over and over. It's hard to give up trying to change something we don't like. But thankfully, my Lord said to come to Him when life gets this way. Now, about having too much of something. I know I've had too much. And right now, the end is not in sight. What to do? For one thing, I can "step back" from the cause, when possible. Rely on dependable other people to do the job. Take a chance to give up trying to determine the outcome, at least for a while. Until rest for the body, mind and soul brings about recovery. But what if dependable people are few, or not even in sight? Such a tiresome plight...to say the very least. So, I must search for some resolve. We know that God does not give us more than we can handle. Seems impossible...but through faith, it is true. But when we are weary we usually don't have too much faith. It's time to dig deep inside. "Here is my belief, help my unbelief." Yes, that brings about some semblance of hope. Just enough to "get us through". God telling us to "hang in there". No, my Lord did not promise me confidence that the problem would be solved or that I'd have great insight. He simply said he would give me rest. Interestingly, I've been humbled to the point in which rest is sufficient for now. Funny...I'm presently convinced with time, the circumstance will eventually unfold...bringing solution. Yes, I have something to look forward to. So, with all being said...there is hope indeed! Gratefulness is due.

"Come unto me, all ye that labour and are heavy laden, and I will give you rest."

Matthew 11:28

The Current Below

It's an undercurrent. Always
a steady flow. It has permanent
residence...existing since the
beginning. A way of life as a
child and adult.

Sometimes heavy, sometimes light.
But forever a weight. There can be
periods of very perplexing balance.

It can be dull. It can be sharp.
Either way there is pain. A pain
which might be rather airy or on
the other hand utterly devastating.

It can be a submergence of terror
and hurt. Torment which may
eventually lead to a numbing effect.

Sometimes it is a typical lethargy.
Other times it may have dark, twisted,
unreal characteristics. A false perception
of being. It may overtake the conscious
and subconscious.

It can make rare appearances, with
reasonable cause. It may go before,
exist in present, or follow behind.
May be all three...at the same time.
Many times not justifiable. It just is.

The fighting...may be just a nuisance.
Or an inner waging of war. Armor
for the battles can well protect...
or provide small, vague assistance.

An all-encompassing worry comes
with "the package". Although, with
fortune, the mind might just briefly
entertain.

It may simply disturb. But it
can wreck existence of person.
Regardless of degree...it is a
very real query.

Some understand. Many have
no idea its intense, negative impact
on the mind, soul, heart and body.

What is this? It is depression.
You say..."You keep beating a dead
horse." Well, yes...the "beating"
continues. What else to do? No
viable option. A "must" for survival.

So, ending this night in the negative?
As stated earlier, it is an ongoing undertow.
Again, at times not so bad. On the
other hand it could lead to premature tragedy.

Understanding it requires listening and
taking action. An inner awareness absolutely
needed to make forward progress. And time.
It takes time to regain composure within.

So it goes with many. Not alone.
Sometimes misunderstood by loved ones.
Possible neglect from friends. But other
times full support is available. Very
grateful and thankful for acknowledgement.

The Fear So Strong

At first guilt and anger. Then recognized as fear that has a grip so tight around the heart and soul. The anxiety so extreme. But then in a flash it's back to guilt and anger. And so the cycle goes. What has brought this on? Lack of knowledge voiced by another. What? Wait, are you casting blame in order to retain composure? Right off the bat...yes. But that's not the answer. No... an assessment must be made in order to retrieve sanity and security. So, how? Well, maybe reassessment is in order to calm the fright. Ok...here goes. A severe problem exists. The victim is riddled with legitimate reasons for thus far not having overcome the problem. But added to that, the individual feels like they have failed. They have not met the standard by which the other has set for them. WHAT THU HELL??!!! WAIT A MINUTE!! DON'T EVEN GO THERE!!! The other has no clue to the magnitude of hell the one is being subjected! How so? Because the adversity is not common among the normal. Hold on. Is that just an excuse for the one to resist a solution? No. It's a fact. A sad fact. That is...a sad fact for such misunderstanding. There are others like this one who suffers in silence, with similar cause. Few...but too many. There is a cry among the reasoning. For sense is not made. Not to the other. And worse, not to the one enduring the strife. How weak the knees and short the breath. Impossible to convey. It must be experienced for true insight of the realm that the agony reaches. So, how to settle on forward motion for the fearful one? At a distance...yes, there is help. It will not come tonight. Nor tomorrow. The wait for resolve. Time, please pass. Fact: No clock stops ticking. Eventually...eventually the answer will surface and the one will at last have relief. In the meantime, let the skin thicken and cling to promise. Despite the odds...you are not alone. By yourself...maybe. But not alone.

Get It Together!

Why? Why on earth keep clouding your judgment? I mean...don't you see the light? Oh, you do...in a way? But still you stay trapped, in what seems to be a business of your own making. Do you get pleasure out of pain? I didn't think so. Well, change! You say it's not that easy? Heard that time and again...coming from those who refuse to face the truth. Hmmm. There seems to be an honesty amidst the conflict. Is this so? Or are you really looking for a way out? Well, I guess you're the only one who truly knows. So be it. I suppose praying for you is in my order. Dare I be so humane? Well, I guess there is a commandment which suggest such. Maybe I better take a look inside. Yep.

Granted...Both Time and Endurance

It is Thanksgiving Eve 2014. Much of significance has occurred in my life this past year. Among other things, it has involved accepting my parents' mortality and seeking to solidify security within myself. I can honestly say that I am steadily working on issues of such magnitude. Progress is slowly being made. Grateful. Just in the last few days, I have looked back at some of my writings from the past two years. I had a lot to say in my work...whether or not it was relevant...well hell, who cares? I got it out of my system! Much to be said for "purging". As I took a second glance at my written expressions, I found two words that kept "coming up" in my writings. The words: Time and Endurance. There are definitely aspects to my person which have not developed fully. As stated in a very important text..."We claim spiritual progress, not spiritual perfection." I have "a ways to go" before I'm where I want to be... with regards to a comfortable "position" in my life. But back to these two words...time and endurance. I have realized that God has granted me time to "get myself together" and endurance to withstand the wait. Wow! That's great! So, I don't "have to have it yesterday!" No. I've been ok with small portions evolving over a fairly lengthy period of time. Have I been impatient at times? Of course. But inside my being, I've held a belief that someday I'll "get there". Yes, I have faith that prayers will eventually be answered and dreams will come true. How refreshing for my soul. Now about "endurance". Man...Some things have been hard. Such struggling along the way. Heights of insanity and depths of despair describe much of my "time". Even so, I've been able to overcome many obstacles and withstand frayed emotions. Indeed, there were times I thought I was totally "losing it". But God...well, He gave me endurance. He saw fit that I did not "drown in sorrows" or "go over the edge". A strength that would eventually calm my anxieties and fears, had developed from defeating prior trials. What blessings I'm reaping!! "A Mighty Fortress", I love that hymn. That's what my God is...a fortress that can "take" whatever is thrown in attempt to destroy. NO! There'll be no destruction here! Problems and pain will come...for sure. But...with God's help, I've developed a true sense of "time" and a voice inside me that proclaims "endurance". It says..."Hang in there. It'll be ok. There'll be relief." Wonderful. "Time and endurance"...the stronghold of survival and soothing hope. Yes. I believe that the perception of these two words, can make a life of conflict and uncertainty turn into an existence carrying a bright future. Indeed, darkness will surround now and then. But a light... there'll be a flame that never dies. And I believe I'll grow. I believe I'll gain and eventually possess security and confidence in the deepest parts of my person. Direction and purpose in life will develop...giving me certain meaning to decisions made. Thanksgiving 2014. Thankful for "time and endurance".

Getting Closer

A change. A break of bad habit.
It's been so very elusive. And so
long the battle. It has taken "self"
captive time and again. Damn its'
power! Damn its' insistence to
control the being.

Longing for "about-face"... seems
forever. Cries...heard? I believe.
But answers revealed? Not as of
present. Discouragement. Yes...
a disheartened spirit always lurks.

But what? You say "getting closer"?
Yes. I think solution will soon be fact.
Time involved? Threw away the clock
long ago. It was only an enemy to the
psyche. A hindrance to the mind...
a mind trying to grasp relief and resolve.

Again..."getting closer"? Again..."yes".
Will it be tonight? Will it be tomorrow?
Don't know. None too soon. Fortunately,
"hopelessness" dropped from the
vocabulary. There was no sense to make
sanity further out of reach. So, pacification
knowing change will indeed eventually
come. And when it does..."HOORAY"!!!!

"Oh Fear...Where Is Thy Sting?"

Look at me God. See the fear?
So overwhelmed. So consumed.
Every part of the body's torso intensely
flutters. Actually, it is more of a hard,
constant, steady pounding. At the very
core, the feel of a dull blade...carving.
No, not despair or sorrow. Not a sinking
state. Not turmoil. Such fright? Yes.

Hear me God? I say...I'm doing my
best to keep pure terror at bay. It is not
black. Rather, the color felt is a deep,
deep brown red. It curses at my being.
How do I escape the trap of living death?
Please God, I cry from the depths. No tears.
Instead, a sickened, vibrating nausea
accompanied by what seems an eternity.

This night, I ask for reprieve. Let it go no
further. There is a bit of faith that you
will release some of the thick vapor of
trepidation. God, can you feel my rapid
pulse? The blood in my body is heavy.
Have mercy. My gut shakes fiercely.
Please tell me the present aura will
eventually dissolve. Remove the grasp
of the surging sense.

Ok. God I've pleaded. You are the answer.
Your response to my plight might come
from the aid of others. That's it. I'm not
alone. That will be the source of which
I draw a semblance of calm. Yes, I have
a minute belief that you can make the hard
beat of the waves lessen and ease.

"Oh Fear...Where Is Thy Sting?"
The answer to the question...presently it
encompasses my person. I tremble as I
scream for resolve in the positive. And
I request more...let relief come soon.
Again, God Have Mercy.

Whoa...What's with the looks?

Ok. The works of the mind can't be seen.
Brainwaves...invisible, we know for a fact.
Thoughts come and go. Sometimes rapidly.
Sometimes stuck. Feelings and emotions...
also lost in the air. The aura can't be touched
with the hand.

But wait. It is possible for the camera to
"catch" a glimpse of sorts...with regards
to the afore-mentioned. Not all the time.
But sometimes the sight is blatant and bold.

What am I getting at? The looks of a mind
and soul that has "taken a beating"...over a
long period of time...indeed there is a tangible
picture. Unfortunately.

How so? A disheveled appearance exists.
There is a "slump" of posture. The same clothes
worn day after day. Many times the daily attire
is also nighttime garb. Wrinkled, with spots and
stains. Easy...throw'em in the washer. Such effort.

Besides a "cut" that doesn't make the most of
features...the hair is oily. Bathing...a chore that seems
impossible to carry out. Time passes and there is
less care. The scent can't be good. And the skin...
so dry.

It is obvious that quality rest and sleep is needed.
"Make-up"...what's that? The teeth...brushing
skipped once in awhile. Needless to say, there
has been no manicure or pedicure. In fact, there
may not be a simple clipping of the nails.

Good God! For heaven's sake...take some pride!
The "indigent look" is never in style. You'd feel
so much better about yourself. Don't you want to
be physically attractive? All you gotta do...
What? You're doing your best just to make it through
the day? Teach me to assume.

Spending The Holidays

Will there be turkey and ham?
How about homemade Christmas candy?
And pies. A variety from which to choose?
A dining table with a "big spread"?
What about a laid-back outdoor meal
reflecting your heritage? For sure, there'll
be "good eats"!

Who's gonna be at the festivities?
Immediate family, relatives, neighbors,
co-workers? Maybe all...staggered
over a two week period. There'll be
people you deeply love, some you simply
like, those only tolerable, and persons you
just flat-out "can't stand".

Decorations. Is the outside of the house
lit up? Or will it be a door wreath and
stockings, at the most? Goes without
saying that an adorned tree will be the
main attraction.

What about gifts? Will they be big or
small? Expensive or cheap? And how
many? Hopefully, lots! Will the wrapping
look like the work of an artist of sorts? Or
will fingerprints show through the Scotch tape?

Going somewhere special...distant...vacation?
"Over the river and through the woods."?
Across town or the house next door? Maybe
the celebration is right at home.

What about religious services? Candlelight
communion? Choir cantatas? Will
"The Reason for the Season" be kept in mind?
Acts of kindness? Will an aura of gentleness
be present? "Good will towards men"?

Music. A Must! Always familiar verses.
Some "light". Some steeped in the Faith.
Coming from shopping malls, church
steeples, television commercials. And of
course, recordings of our favorites played
on electronic devices.

Children. Demanding the center of attention
in a desirable fashion. Aren't they the most
important to please? They furnish laughter,
crying, delightfulness. Their absolute belief in
stories which bring awe...it's "catching". The
old find themselves starting to believe...even
when they know better.

Oh my...what to wear? Which sweater...
green or red? Lots of "bling"? Or the casual
look? Naturally, it will depend on the event
to be attended. High hopes that Santa will bring
more clothing...and accessories. JEWELRY!

What if all the afore-mentioned is not present?
How can it really be Christmas or New Year's?
Only strangers around. Institutional food.
The few decorations have to comply with safety
codes. Visits with others...last an hour at the most.
Perhaps there is no company of friends or family.
No sounds of jovial tunes. Moans of despair, fright
and sadness are what is heard. Enough.

Ok. So is sympathy sought in such an atmosphere?
Maybe to a degree. But it doesn't last long. For
the pain...the reason for the circumstance, it persist.
Thoughts are geared towards survival. It's just
another day filled with inner conflict and turmoil.

So bleak. There can't be any meaning of "holiday"
for the tormented soul. OH, BUT NOT SO!
It is The Father, The Son, The Spirit...The
"Three In One". It is the substance that one tightly
holds onto day in, day out. This Being...God,
the very essence and purpose for the designated
days of rejoicing. Forever and Wherever!
Always!

Words vs. Feelings

Fear in the gut. A tired being...
yet sleep despised. Wondering.
Wondering where a path will lead.
To not know. How it can fright.

Old ways. For the most part, their
protection has fallen. A tearing
down of habits which hid. So naked.
So cold. And the apprehension rises.

Feelings raw, unmasked. So dangerous.
Dangerous to the sense of security.
To feel. Not to speak. Experience
without written expression. Scary.

The reason for such foul senses...
not known. Oh...the vague view
of the inner self...can bring about
mild terror. Has to be halted.

Uncomfortable, undesirable emotions
attempting to overwhelm. One has
learned...words can express, but they
can also hide. A resource to prevent
intense attack of strange despair.

Feelings slowly escalating to heights...
no longer clothed by customary methods
of preservation. To "feel"...no speech.
At least no vocalization which searches
for rescue. Rather, with sight strained...
looking at "what is". Terrific trepidation.

No. No words. The battle of "feel".
Can be so tumultuous. Direction of
walk not given. But it must be, in
order to find. To find the elusive resolve.

What to do in the wait? While a frightful
misery exists...what to do? Go back.
Not to be mistaken with "backwards".
Store away the "breaks" in sanity.
Retreat, as to remain undefeated.

For now...step into the familiar.
It holds safety. A calm is needed
while biding time. Say it. Put words
in motion. Get a grip on what was once
reality. Hold tight. Yes, write what is
felt. Let the "unveiled feel" take a back
seat in the mind, body and soul.

The pen. The type. The salvation.
And so, on this night...a night of fragile
uncertainty...let the words flow.

"Hightail It"

Run! Get outta here!
Away from a new reality.
Facts not known...but dreaded.
Not sure the "fight or flight" is
really necessary. But taking
precautions.

Where to go? Treat yourself...
somewhere nice. A bright beam.
A rainbow. A clean flowing river.
Now, those are desirable. We
have to believe...it's possible

What else? The end to fault in
self. Let go. Needless cargo.
Indeed, make the journey "light".
It's a choice at this point. Make
it be. Make it be more than tolerable.
That's it! Make it enjoyable!

The ride. Everyone has their road.
Some dirt, some gravel, some paved.
Smooth travel in life...we all want.
Why not right now? Yes, things
are good. Really...half-empty, half-full?

Shout HOORAY!!! Rejoice in all
the positives. Don't just "see the light
at the end of the tunnel". No, in fact
don't even enter into the darkness in the
first place. More than "stay the course".
Instead, follow a new map. A fun route.

All this...is it possible to turn misery
into a pleasant intoxicating fragrance?
I believe. YES! I believe of the
possibility. But action must be taken.
Walk away...refrain from returning.

Am I gonna be someone special this
night? Yes. I'll be in "the winner's
circle". Claiming the prize. You say
you have gifts for me? That there can
be a new "air"? Steps in forward dance?

All sounds good. But by what authority?
Who are you that can grant such?
Oh...Now I can see you God! My...
such promise!

Conflict Trumps Disregard

Why the hell do you do this to yourself?
Can't you just "let be"? Accusations within.
Blaming self for actions. Actions and
reactions which only seem to bring
calamity to the soul.

To look inside and see such uncertainty.
Questioning the "reasons for". And getting
no answer. Intimidation, brought on by
self-inflicted distrust. All due to a lack of
healthy love for one's person.

Why try to sort through wreckage?
Just dismiss the fact that there has been no
rational cause. You're only "going in circles".
The reason may never present itself. Do you
have an affinity for torture? It appears.

In reply: A wholeness is sought. Positive
resolution is desired. Peace. Yes...the want
for a deeper peace. Solidity. The foundation
is there, but reinforcement is necessary to
be at ease. Indeed...seeking "a calm".

Therefore, investigation is a must. Fear in
the quest...always. Confronting stagnation.
So hard. Walking the path is far from simple.
What will be found? Can it be faced without
loss of security of the known? That is, what's
known to be fancied for well-being.

God Have Mercy. Let there be "a find".
Don't let "the unearthed" be greater than
positive existence. Asking for solution
to invisible problems. Can't be seen...
but oh my, how pronounced the fear.

So, onward. Walking into and out of.
Strengthen and bring a growing sense
of certainty. That being certain, good.
I believe. It will come. One day
persecution of the being will die. A
grave will then confine the destroyed.

Not yet. No. A settlement denied
so far. But there is faith. There is hope.
The "seeking" will be rewarded. One
will lay claim to a life of much more
appreciation and love. Loving self
with "no strings attached". And no ropes
binding. Someday soon.

Life On The Border

But it has always been. At least
for the most part. A border that
prevents complete definition of self.
Of course there may be description,
but it is tainted by fierce emotion.

The remains of a reason, darken
the pleasing self-worth that one has
established. How minute are the
desirable aspects called to attention.
And the only person making the
call is inside.

The auras. Such discomfort they
produce. Not only undesirable...
but the border has become a
breeding ground for terror.
Please...release!

Beliefs built on flawed and false
perception, ignite flames of guilt.
The border keeps out fluid motion
of life and some serious security.
There may be safety with regards
to many issues. But doubts run
rampant in some corners.

How to overcome? Delving.
But before the "dig", nets on which
to land must be in place. The recall
of the good has to be a part of the look
inside.

So it is...life on the border. Unsuspecting,
unexpected...many of the darts thrown.
The points can be very piercing. Painful.
Actual blindness to the cause probably
exists. Making for an extremely troubled
mind. Some violent physical reaction
possible, when senses are aroused.

But there is hope. There is help. One allows
another to enter the locked room...carefully.
Trust is established. A trust absolutely
necessary for freedom to express.

Walking a tight rope and looking down.
Not good. Must rely on taking steps
instinctively. It will come. Yes. One day
the bottom will be reached. Not in a bad
sense...but as "a way out". And the bird
will take flight. Can never be too soon.

And Yet...I "Cuss"

Let's get this straight from the beginning. I'm a native Southeast Texan...and I live in Arkansas. The word is "cuss" not "curse". With that clarification...I'll proceed.

I say kind words to others...and yet I cuss.
I do good deeds...and yet I cuss.
I obey the law...and yet I cuss.
I proclaim God's love...and yet I cuss.
I care for my parents...and yet I cuss.
I am honest...and yet I cuss.
I respect humanity...and yet I cuss.
I carry out my responsibilities...and yet I cuss.
I treat people fairly...and yet I cuss.
I understand the meaning of the foul words...and yet I cuss.
I never heard profanity come from my childhood home...and yet I cuss.
I do not wish ill will when I say such, most of the time...and yet I cuss.
I know "it's not becoming of a lady"...and yet I cuss.

Well, enough...you get the message. So why do I cuss? Because it FEELS GOOD!!!

Do I go "overboard" and "make a scene" in public when I express myself in this manner? Oh...there have been a few occasions when I wanted to hide afterwards. But

for the most part I use such speech rather carefully...
for the most part. Do I feel like God does not want
me to say "words of color"? Yes. Do I usually ask
Him for forgiveness when all is said? Yes. And yet...I
cuss again. Am I a hypocrite? Well...in a way...I guess
so. And yet...I continue to cuss. Do I truly regret this
verbalization? Well...let's face it...only momentarily.
And yet...I cuss once more.

With all that's been said...should I "straighten up
my act"? One would think so. Do I want to change?
Ok...honestly..."no". Why? Why continue what is
considered a "sin" of sorts? BECAUSE It's Such a
Relief and Release of tension and stress. Not only
that...IT'S FUN !!!! You ask...why is it so fun? I don't
know. Maybe I like being a bit "edgy". Maybe I like to
"go against" my upbringing. Maybe I like that some
words can more aptly describe a particular situation
or person. But again...let's just downright face it...It's
So Gratifying! A type of "exorcism". A "cleansing"...
no not in the sense of purity. But a "getting it out of the
system". A "habit"...perhaps a "bad habit".

Ok. So you who are appalled by this writing...there is a
type of redemption. I DO feel a bit of guilt. AND YET...I
CUSS!!! Oh well...for tonight, I'll just ignore "right and
wrong"...and say "I Don't Give A Rat's Ass!!!" But the
conscience creeps...UGH!!!!

A Calm Soul

Dead? No. Depressed? No.
What's the matter? Matter being
substance. So, what's the substance
that causes the quiet inside?

Damn. Why inquire? Just go with
the flow. Presently, there is no
adversity. Leave well enough alone!

But at the core...there is not a settlement.
There are questions to be answered.
Reasons...not known. In all likelihood,
they will have to be resolved for forward
movement.

Even though clarity and solution are not
in the day's equation...it is alright.
What's that?... "It is well with my soul."
Yes, inside and out...there is a smoothness.
So strange to this one who always seems to
be riding a roller coaster.

There is a small amount of caution, among
what is thought might be an inner tease.
Stop. Just let be. Listen to the heart beat.
It's beating in a slow, steady rhythm.
Allow that sound to continue to pervade
the mind. The mind, so often in torment.

Be thankful. Sing a song of praise.
For now...let soft air fill and encompass.
It is a gift. "A break in the action."
Give credit where credit is due...
"Be still and know that I am God."

"Unwrap The Present!"

You don't have to wait till Christmas.
Even though it evolved during the
Celebration Season, it is a year round
gift. Everybody is given the present.
You just have to accept and receive.

The wrapping paper. It's a beautiful
sight. Strange that bloodstains produce
a redness. Red...a holiday color.
And that paper...it's more like a cloth.
A shroud. Paper or cloth, it covers a
special "favor".

How much did it cost...you ask?
Well...for One it was most expensive.
Yes. Indeed, an ultimate price was paid.
But for you and me...It's Free!
Just like most Christmas gifts we
are given.

Who is "doing the giving"?
Someone who knows just what
you want...just what you need.
All knowing. Always in the midst.
The giver happens to be a maker.
Making the gift. Making you and me.

Well...go ahead, open it! Tear off
the wrapping! Act like a child.
What's inside? I'll bet it's what I found...
a Son shining. Giving a warmth that
is so desperately needed. And it's a
"type" of friend...who loves unconditionally!

Along with the "sweater of sorts", comes a
security...a guarantee...an eternal warranty.
And The Spirit of the season can be felt!
Yes. The Christmas Spirit! A Holy Spirit!
Angels are singing. We can join the caroling.

Mary had a part in this "Merry Christmas".
Our gift...her infant Son, He attracts
both simple animals and men of wise.
This holiday...Unwrap The Present!
And claim it! It can be all yours, forever!!

Patience for the Feat

Will it ever happen? When will
it be solved? Is there going to
be resolve...for once? Not with
this type. But "yes"...there is hope.
In small increments there is belief
and faith.

What happens in the meantime?
Perhaps doubts bring about guilt.
Not doubts that the obstacle can be
overcome. Instead, guilt stemming
from doubts of worthiness. Yes...trying
to avoid the feeling of "falling short".

So, will the ill will towards self, bring
an extremely unpleasant conflict within?
Only if allowed. Yes, there is control
over mind-set...at least to a degree.
But why? Why can't what seems simplistic
be "straightened-out"? Or...is it so simple?

It didn't "happen overnight". This curse
which throttles well-being. Oh...if it
could just be gone. Go Away! Get
out of here! Well...it's not leaving.
No. Not yet.

Wait. All is not a loss. There is good.
Yet, a sense of insanity weaves in the gut.
What to do with the fluctuation of thoughts
and feelings? Sometimes good. Sometimes
bad. A lot of time, survival instinct "steps in"
in order to bring order. A feeling of "hang on"
is the best that can be achieved at present.

So, at this moment there will be no solution.
What to do? Lighten up. Find the positive.
Oh...so much easier said than done! Enough.
Again...find the forward motion. Yes, going
in the right direction. Let that be enough for
right now. Godspeed...Please!

The Feel Of "Down"

The feel of down...fear.

The feel of down...nausea.

The feel of down...worry.

The feel of down...regret.

The feel of down...sorrow.

The feel of down...physical pain.

The feel of down...inner pain.

The feel of down...absence.

The feel of down...neglect.

The feel of down...lonely.

The feel of down...alone.

The feel of down...mistakes.

The feel of down...unacceptance.

The feel of down...wet, wet tears.

The feel of down...reminders.

The feel of down...memories.

The feel of down...abuse.

The feel of down...outcast.

The feel of down...turmoil.

The feel of down...reprimand.

The feel of down...material poverty.

The feel of down...conflict.

The feel of down...handicaps.

The feel of down...loss.

The feel of down...incomplete.

The feel of down..."the joke of".

The feel of down...disrespect.

The feel of down...disappointment.

The feel of down...bleak future.
The feel of down...tired.
The feel of down..."lied to".
The feel of down...rejection.
The feel of down...death.
The feel of down...guilt.
The feel of down...tremble.
The feel of down...unappreciated.
The feel of down...shame.
And on and on...

The settling of a repulsion in the gut, when "down" is felt.
How we so hurt, when we feel "down".
Cause, insignificant at the height of "down".
"A way out"...not visible when "down".
Tender touch can't be felt when "down".
Destination doomed...when "down".
Gloom forever present when "down".
Such a lack of control when "down" is felt.
Words of wisdom are not heard when "down".
Vision is blurry when "down".
Senseless words are muffled, as we try to voice when "down".

"Lifting Up" a requirement for desired "brotherly love".
To "Lift Up" a responsibility of every human being.
And every soul who reads, as well as the writer...We must take heed!

What Is This? Faith?

What keeps us going? What makes us endure? How do know there is a light at the end of the tunnel... when in fact, we're not even sure we're in a tunnel? How can we ever experience solace, when we keep running from it? Forever...answers vague and for the most part unknown...in the human sense. So, we have to look beyond our own abilities to survive. Because basically, our ability is extremely limited. At least when it comes to such undefined gray aura, circling around our head. Oh...how we dread the thought of that lighter shade turning black. But Wait. Don't go that route. It leads to more and more helplessness. Causes unknown, convictions unsettled. Then what direction should we take? So far, we have met nothing but a brick wall. Let's think outside of the tragic perception of self. There appears in print and is heard from voice..."Faith". A belief that the unknown will eventually be of a positive nerve. Not to be...not yet. But soon...yes, I believe soon. Bells will ring with a thrill of life. Perspectives will lead to a desirable feel. We will be encompassed with pleasing satisfaction. How? What matter has been afforded us the true right for certainty, when appearances are so bleak? A Spirit. A Being within our being. It says "Yes, you can do it". We begin to experience a pride about possibilities once thought not relevant. We "cling". Holding onto whatever course of surety develops. It is a speck. It certainly seems all too tiny to grow worthy of notice.

But again...Wait! It can happen...a miracle. There will be answers to questions...questions lacking our own understanding. That's right...we "mouth" words which we are not certain to hold truth. And we do this by way of...Faith. We can't see it. We can't touch it. We can't hear it. BUT eventually, we come to Know It. It is said that the greatest is Love. And I believe that to be true. But Faith...it's right there in its company. Oh... did I forget Hope? Yep...it goes along with these other qualities which require action. What action? Actually, it takes very little action...for it is "surrender". We "let go". We "turn over". We "give to". Yes, surrendering is the beginning of Faith. And the more we surrender, the more faith grows. I trust this night and morn has not been in vain. A sense of relief has begun to ease a burden. Rescued from our weighted souls, we begin to feel the Spirit rise. Oh God in heaven lift us higher and higher! I have faith in You! And You give me faith in myself. Thank You.

Customizing Insanity

Gonna do it my way. It's crazy.
So what? What the hell? If I'm
gonna "lose it"...have fun at it!!
Rules, standards, "do what's best".

Well, I hear the precautions. I know
the consequences. Am I walking on
a high wire with no net below? No.
Not that extreme. But I am "bucking
the system". Whose system? Well,
my system.

So...in other words I'll pay the price
if there is a cost? Yes. Is this a
grave situation? Only if I let it be.
Damn...just "blow it off"! You
take yourself way too seriously!
My mind's jungle is only as dense
as I allow.

So, look at the "bright". Knock
down the negative. Sure you'll
probably feel a little bit like shit.
But goodness...make "light". Don't
despair when the "feel" is uneasy.
And don't make the uneasy "eerie".
That IS in your control!

So is it "insane"? Well, kinda.
But must grief accompany the
unconventional...at least what you
consider not "the norm"? Honestly,
it doesn't have to.

Does it sound as if I'm "goin' out on
the town and tyin' one on"? Sorta.
But that's FAR from reality. No...
I'm safe and sound. Well...in a way,
I'm not using very sound judgment.

But really, I know what's comin'…
and I know what's goin'. And what's
"goin'" is NOT gonna be my sanity.
NO...not anymore!!! You readers...
you dyin' to know what the heck I'm
talkin' about? Not gonna tell ya.
Doesn't amount to a "rat's ass" anyhow!

On The Light Side...On The Bright Side

If things are "light", things can be
"bright". Why let darkness win at
a game that's not really being played
with intensity?

What is the "measuring stick" of
intensity? Perhaps "perspective".
Importance, relevance...what makes
it so? Maybe how one feels.

Feelings...ahh. So shifty. Such
ambivalence much of the time.
How can we ever place our lucidity
on emotions? Dare fright overcome
our person, when comfort dissipates?

So, we "go with it". Throw guilt,
shame, regrets out the window. We've
made our bed. It's ours...we sleep in it.
Again...so uncomfortable. But no...
no more fear even when other feelings
are "creepy".

But let's get back to the "light".
Light-heartedness. A big word...
a delightful word. Frivolity?
Maybe. Despair nowhere to be
found in such word.

Ok..."light" sounds good. And
"bright light" sounds even better.
It's right in front. There for the
taking. Gonna grab hold. Relief,
gladness, happy, boldness, certainty.
No more "deer in the headlights"!

When "The Scare" Is Gone

The previous day and night...
such fear overwhelmed.
Instructions given to quiet
the frightful desperation.
A choice made which made
the present "good and safe".

Now...again faced with decision.
How different this night. Filled
with well-being, it is harder to
make the "right" choice. Not just
"right", but "wise".

Think, think, think. Not in the
sense of repetitious bullshit. No...
remember. Recall the emotion that
was so consuming and dangerous.
For a moment relive the sense
of lack of control, experienced as
a result of "poor choice".

How our memory of "bad" can
fade, when "good" is in place.
False confidence prevails.
A "change of habit" is the issue.
The only way to break the
cycle which brings suffering is
to make that "wise" choice.

So, what's it gonna be? Gonna
"set self up" for a dismal, following
day...which will eventually lead to
the dreaded existence?

Consider truth. Consider reality.
Don't turn your back on what
certainty lies ahead. Talk to
yourself minus the present good
feeling. Remember, remember,
remember outcomes. Yes,
remember...don't give yourself
the luxury to consider. You're
too irresponsible. Enough.

To Not Despair

To not despair...write.
Times much better...yet.
Thoughts not as cursed...yet
Emotions more settled...yet.
What then do you want?
The world? No.

Not looking for perfection.
Material wealth not a goal.
Instead...a symptom relieved.
Yes. That's what's sorely desired.

Oh...but so much has already
been accomplished. But
more needed to ease conflict
within...bringing outward
positive change.

Must you? Must you make
"big" out of "small"? Not true.
Complex and very real, this
adversity. Could it be worse?
By all means...yet.

The battle continues with the write.
The words are protection. An
avoidance they offer. But they
will come to a close. Leaving what?
Leaving the unsolved riddle naked.

A fright accompanies. Sometimes
strong...sometimes mild. Oh...
Get a grip! Trying. Some success...
then two steps back. Damn it...
be done with such coarse introspection.

Wait. This night there is no delving...
only feeling. And it is not a mood.
It is a flare. To extinguish, impossible.
So what to do to "get by"? Can't be
ignored...as it engulfs.

Just trying to "make it". Will there be
an answer? Again...at this point, not
looking for reason. Don't have to
understand. Only ask for removal
of such thorn for the time being.

Ok ego. Let go. Obviously, it is
not your load to handle. Then whose?
Get real! Get honest! Get on your knees!
But that's been tried. Tonight? Well...
not really. Instead there has been a
paralyzing effort. Leading only to
more intensified discomfort.

Well then...reach out once more.
And stop "beating yourself up"!
It is not your fault. But it is your
decision to make. Are you gonna
"give it away"? Or hold on and
compound the apprehensive misery?

Oh must I? Must I relinquish control of self...all of self? It's so opposite this internal drive. Keep on...more troubling abounds. Ok...here goes...

God in Heaven, please forgive, save and fill. Relieve the inner pressure. In your name. Now...end the write.

Is It Because We Are Weak?

Is it because we are weak? This failure to overcome what has become a huge obstacle. I mean it's gone on and on for more than one calendar. When will there be an answer? When will there be "a way out"? When will there be resolve? And the answer...right now..."Don't know". The problem seems rather ridiculous...kinda insane. It is innocent...but "the devil". Much turmoil, fear and grief this albatross has brought to our everyday life. It is a "constant". Impossible for forward movement, thus far. We are truly stuck in a quandary. Ok...enough. This write has expressed the situations' power adequately. So, what to do? There have been many avenues approached, with beliefs to rectify the situation. But to no avail. Why haven't we been able to change the predicament? Why? Is it because we are weak? Weak-willed? I'm guessing...No. In fact, I'm positive...No. Just because we fail and fail to progress doesn't necessarily mean we are a "powerless individual". On the contrary. In fact, it shows that we are actually very strong because we have survived. We have endured. We've "taken a beating" and are still standing. Oh...we may sway, but we are standing. Ok... sometimes we may even "sit down" or "lay down"... but eventually we "get back up". Damn the pain involved!! Is it fair? Do we deserve such? Those two questions are not even in the equation. So, just dismiss that line of thinking. It's called "Life". However bizarre, it's all part of a "master plan". Oh...don't EVEN go there! What's that? Lack of faith. Well, that's Nowhere near the truth! We can have an abundance of faith and continue to falter. Faith in ourselves, others and yes... even faith in God. But still...what has become a type of torture, continues. So, again...what to do? We accept. What?!! Yes, we accept. Does this mean we "settle"? Are we just going to give up...stop trying to change the adversity? NO! It simply means we take our present state...and continue to breathe. Yes, life goes on despite the conflict. Ok...but so unpleasant are our days. Can we continue to hold on? "In steps" Hope! We cling to "hope" that one day we WILL be "free". Is "hope" something less than "faith"? Well, the only answer... it's in good company. "Faith, hope and love"...so goes the verse. We hope for better days. No...We hope for "The Best" of days! Why not? We're due such. Indeed!

What Is Heaven Gonna Be Like?

Eternity. Heaven. What's it really gonna be like? It doesn't matter whether you're a Bible scholar or someone who is only familiar with John 3:16. Either way, you don't know any more than I do. SO...that leaves it up to my imagination. First of all, let me clarify, I believe there will be much praising and singing to our Maker. But is that ALL it's gonna be? I mean, honestly, that alone sounds kinda boring. We're promised it will be paradise. Isn't paradise many times different for each individual? Certainly. With that being said...here's what I'm looking forward to. I think it will be great to be reunited with all my pet animals. Do you realize how CROWDED heaven is gonna be with everybody's pets?!!! Not to mention all the "strays"! Whoa!! Then I believe I'll have a sound proof room with a recliner, in which I can listen to ALL my favorite music...as loud as I want. In that room there'll be plenty of space for friends to come and dance, dance, dance. AND I'll be coordinated in my dance...Yes, I'll have rhythm...at last!! I won't be making a fool of myself! Then there's my sports. Once again, I'll be "in shape" and can participate. I'll hit homeruns in the rebuilt Astrodome. I'll score over 30 points in pro basketball games. Making the game-winning basket "at the buzzer" occasionally! And FOOTBALL FOR GIRLS!!!!!! YES!!!!! A dream!! To top it off... I'll get to attend as many College Baseball World Series as I desire. And my teams will win. Won't that be great...the Lamar Cardinals...NCAA Baseball

Champions!!! Well...I hope heaven "pans-out" to be so spectacular. I believe it will. Of course, my earthly imagination can never conceive the unbelievable fun and enjoyment we'll all experience...FOREVER!!! OH YEAH...I forgot...ICE CREAM!!! All I want...without weight gain!!!!!!!! Nope...sure don't want to miss out on what is to be for me! And you too, can have your own paradise! (By the way...this was written in all sincerity.)

To Change

Desiring the better...no the Best!
Can it become such in this life?
In the past, the corridor has been
dark. Remnants of ghosts, faults,
fears, doubts...most of the time
undermining the "good times".

No More! A new perspective.
No longer hesitation to be fair
and good to self. "Pumping-up"
only for a downfall? Don't think
so. Certainly there will be question.
Goes with the territory.

Well, what will bring about this
change in demeanor? Answers to
questions? Maybe not. It may never
be explained...so be it. How to
"about-face" if reason not known?

Allow methods never before used.
I mean...really try to "let go" of
old ways. Ways which haven't been
working. As so often stated...
"The definition of insanity is doing
the same thing over, expecting
different results."

What about another saying...
"Is the glass half-empty or half-full?"
That's a stinger! Oh...how we can
live on a steady diet of pessimism.
Time to see the glass filled to the
brim. And ready to drink.

A challenge? Yes. But already small
steps have been taken...with desirable
finds. There is a belief that further
forward movement will be established...
albeit a bit weak. But just "a bit".
Growth, however minute...take it.

So, this early morning, what will be
the verdict? Will we "beat ourselves
over the head"...due to what seems to
be change so insignificant? NO!
Every inch counts! The sum...it will
add up to a substantial amount.

And let go. Let the demons out.
More than that..."usher" them out.
Make space for the good. Renew
a spirit that has never existed.
That seems like a contradiction.
Hell...life so far has been one big
contradiction. So it goes.

The future. Ahh...the future.
It starts right now...at this moment.
Will there be shades of guilt and
conclusions of failure? Damn It! NO!
Ok. Then look at the upcoming hour.
What to do? What to think? The
problem has not been solved. It's ok.
Time is on the side of good.

Understanding Struggle

Problems. We all have them.
Some of the load "heavy"...
some "light". Some...mild conflict.
Others...rampant chaos. Yes, we
all struggle. What to do? What to
say? What to think?

Most of the time when we "battle",
we want to understand the force of
which we are opposing. If it's external,
we look around us, hoping to see the
source. If it's internal...I'm talkin' bout
deep down internal...we just plead for
a moment of relief.

So much we don't comprehend...
concerning both ours and others' struggles.
At times when another's are confounded...
oh, we can so clearly see solution.
But then it happens to us. Lord forbid
anyone give their opinion!! They don't
really understand...we profess.

Let's cut through the bullshit! We're all
different. Who are we to suppose we
can actually put ourselves in another's
shoes? Fact is...we can't even tie our
own shoe strings!! When we try to
assume reason or force a resolve that
carries an "attitude"...where does it get us?
What does it do for our brother? More strife.

Well then, how do we understand each other's
troubles? Oh...in some ways we can "relate".
Maybe we've experienced similar situations.
We "found our way out". Why can't they
just do what we did to solve? Basically,
they just want attention, or don't have the
gumption to get out of their dire straits.
How dare we think such!

Again, how do we understand the complex?
I believe it's got to start with compassion.
In fact, through the whole course of another's
predicament, it may be the only thing we
are capable of offering. We might just need
to "shut-up" and put our arm around them.
Yes, at times the human touch can bring
about healing, rather than words of which
even we ourselves don't know the definition.

So, we may never truly understand our fellowman's struggles. We are all so unique. Our actions, reactions, thoughts...they all differ. Am I saying "Don't even try to understand and help?" By no means. We should do our best to feel their heart and soul. Perhaps pertinent suggestion is appropriate. And hey...sometimes a bit of confrontation based in true care is necessary.

But back to compassion. It is the beginning and "rides to the end". Always needed in our relations with one another. Are we willing to let what can be "haughty" aspirations of proclaiming our opinions...can we "snuff out" such critical thought? We must...to begin to understand another's struggles. Again, our shoulder to cry on...may produce the most comfort. A comfort that we all need. Compassion...never to be underestimated.

Future Optimism or Optimistic Future

Future optimism or optimistic future.
What a choice! One can either see the good
to be of a hopeful prediction, or grasp the
belief that the future will indeed be positive.
And the future begins in the present. Right now!

Where are you? Where am I?
With only the ability to speak for self,
the desire to believe optimism is already
taking place in the present...yes, that's
what I want. I don't want to wait for the
future to bring desirable life. I've been
bound long enough.

I've heard about the promise of abundant life.
Well, that's optimistic. But only if I take
action to reach for the heights said guaranteed.
A disposal necessary. Yes, let go of the trash.
Wandering around in an unpredictable, predictable
maze of misery. Don't want that anymore.

Back to the "Optimistic Future". Ok...the time
is at hand to claim what can be a glory. First I
have to believe I deserve good. Sometimes the
acquisition of such perspective calls for admission
that what was thought true...is actually false.
No. Nobody has lied to me. It is of my own making.
The trap of holding onto harmful ways, trying to
feel safe. Crap! That's a glaring contradiction!

Ok. Enough explanation of a statement I feel so profound. Oh my gosh...check out my ego!!! Speaking of which, the ego...in the past it has been crushed. Not of my own doing. But now, now is different. Revelations, insights of worth have begun to establish a solid base of optimism. And I need to build on that base. Won't happen by itself.

So on this night, how optimistic am I? Well, I'm gettin' there. Oh, come on...you can do better than that! You've voiced such promise, now actually "walk the walk". Ok...if I can take it one step at a time. Ridiculous!!! Jump into the good! It's up to you...the future can remain in the future. Or motion forward to claim prizes, can immediately commence. Yep. It's up to me. No excuses.

Reddish-Orange

Colors of the rainbow...how they're glorified.
But rain came first. And gray was the picture.
Part of the cycle of everyday life. No doubt
the shades can be more or less intense...
according to the depth of the scene being
painted. Sometimes light. Sometimes heavy.
So it goes.

Long ago it was "pitch black". It was before
a comprehension of reality. Terror. Horrifying
despair. And yet, thought normal. To know
different...impossible. Then when totally
broken...an intervention slowly unveiled
the color wheel. The artist began to have
the ability to paint with shades of joy.
Endless gratitude.

And what about recent artwork? Definitely
not rainbows with pots of gold. Did the deep
dark consume? No. Thank God. So what
about the color? Reddish-orange. Oh...there
were streaks of black...but not demonic.
Red, orange and some gray.

The canvas...a battlefield. Fireworks of pain.
Cannons, guns, smoke, brown bloody earth.
The fallen...some dead. Others "hanging-on"
in the misery. Perhaps wishing for death.
Guts exposed. Literally? No. But the ache...
so excruciating that the physical body was
tortured with each breath.

This battle of the war...how long did it last?
Four to five days and nights. Oh...there was
fighting prior and afterward. But the intolerable,
intensified hell...several days. There was question
by all when reprieve would occur. In fact, some
wondered if release of torment possible. Silence,
except for the occasional cry..."God have mercy."

The fifth day...the grip around the soul eased.
Just a bit...but enough to grant some hope. Then
it was all "clockwork". Yes...bide time. Slowly,
over days...yes...God had mercy. Tired and
weary from combat...much rest required.
What about the color? Now a soft, pale blue.
Breathing relaxed. Belief that once more all
colors will be available to paint a life worth
living. God is good.

Whispers So Loud

The crying...annoying and irritating.
The uncontrollable screams...perhaps false alarms.
The harried scuffling...so disjointed.
The words...unpredictable and coarse.
Whispers of despair hardly heard, save the souls
who dare to listen.

The heart beats heavy, as the pulse flushes rapidly
through the body. A never-ending extreme discomfort.
Eyes gaze through the fog of human lens. Bizarre.
Sounds...their impact so strong...bring loud obnoxious
pain. And yet others don't seem bothered by the fright.

There is a wailing inside. Is it the result of death?
No. Has the heart been broken? No. Basic needs
not met? No. Expectations fallen short? No.
What then? What could possibly flaunt such an
enemy to breath? What? Speak up...whispers only
minimize the true threat to sanity.

A crisis occurring...day in, day out. The mind has
been ravaged...no mercy to be found.
Limp motion...must be the result of careless living.
Paying the price for disregard? No. How can it be
that such intrusion on peace evolves, if thought
is indeed innocent? Surely it is deserved...how else
can it be explained?

Such as it is...sometimes no understandable explanation. No rational reason...bringing disgust to the onlooker. Stand up straight. Gather the loose strings. What? Impossible? Yes. Those cries and screams...the uncontrollable scuffle and speech...can't be bridled? No. It is out of reach for the scrambled brain.

Wait! Stop the wreckage from impeding the totality of function. Yes...there is help...there are the select few who can confiscate what is left of the beaten. Reach out. Even in fear...reach out. Allow another to redirect. Give up control? Yes...for the moment. There is no shame...rather, bravery.

There is the calm. Tranquility. Purpose. Clarity. These properties have been sorely missed. A refreshing "new". Strength, power, and common sense begin to surface. There is a grand welcoming to order. And God? Yes. The ultimate orchestrator of revitalization. The Spirit of comfort, belief, hope. Possibly not felt or noticed during the agony. And yet... always present in the midst of decay. Always carrying.

So, rest. And in time resume the walk on a positive path. Packing security, resilience, and freedom. Strides will be greater with less complication. What about joy? That will come in due time. For now...the immediate benefit...the ability to relax and breathe easier. A quaint prize? NO! Instead the very root from which all other wonderful and cherished laurels will develop and grow.

Now...share. Share the possibility of relief, desire for life, and attainment of goals. No need to hide the defeat... it is the beginning of an unimaginably greater victory!

Night and Day

What is the difference between night and day?
"Creative flow." Once a "night owl", the writing
abounded. Now there is the much needed
sleep. Such an answer to prayer. The once
insane fight was so intense, and the voice
wanted to be heard. But what now?
Can't the "overcoming" be expressed with
positive tone? Surely God's deliverance
should be praised.

So what about this hour? Four o'clock...too early
for rise. Yet this morn, after ample slumber,
language began to resonate. To lay with a
ceaseless inner sound, forming explanation
to the present, seemed such a waste. Thus
the type ensued.

The past work...hardship had been much
of the source. But with it came such
fulfillment and satisfaction. The strain
had not been all negative. Experiencing
the passion involved...most of the time
exhilarating. A "natural high".

The future? It is "a definite"...no desire to
return to the old. But the delight of seeing
"written structure" of the mind brings
enjoyment. Satisfaction and purpose produced.
Careful! Don't want to trip and stumble.
How to prevent such a fall? Of course...
like all of life...leave the "creative flow"
at the feet of the Creator!

Seeing Hurt, Through Healed Eyes

The fright. The sadness. Head hung
down as a reprieve from stimulus.
Attempts to coerce relief, a smile, or
any semblance of ease are futile.

The fear...what is the cause? A nightmare?
Confusion? Same surroundings...which are
foreign and new again and again. The plague
on memory disassembles any attempt to
reassure. No response to words or touch.

The sad...a hurting of the soul is evident.
Not many tears. How deep is the pain when
emotion can't be thoroughly expressed.
Some whimpers are audible. A reaction of
comfort would seem appropriate and humane.
But efforts are useless...the unknown surpasses.

To see the loved suffer...hard...very hard.
For so many years the roles were reversed.
How did they survive the pain they witnessed?
Silence guilt...no one at fault. It has been the
lives lived. Nothing more...nothing less.
Life on life's terms.

A belief. A trust. A Comforter.
"Seek ye first the kingdom of God and His righteousness. And all these things shall be added unto you." Hope for the future.
An eternity where Heaven is the playground!

And So Life Goes

So much peace. So much resolve. Happiness.
And so life goes. The pieces of the puzzle fit...
lacking one. Oh my, I thought things were going
good. Yes, that is a fact. And so grateful. But...
But what? Perhaps it is time to fight till I'm totally
free. Actually, the fight began at birth. Battles,
wars, scars, devastation. All the while, reprieve
would come and go. What hinges? God's approval.

Despite concealment of inner self by a protesting
acknowledging self, the conflict thrived. It's <u>not</u>
what it is! Too Evil! The thought repulsive. So
unacceptable. Oh, there has been delving, searching
for resolve...all these years. And yet, a complete
peace...evasive. Surely, there is exaggeration in this
write. Absolutely Not! It plows through the deepest
part of the soul. Rocking the core of identity with
the most severe of repercussions.

Some sides say "right". Some sides say "wrong".
But when it comes down to it...it is for me to
"give the nod"...or not. Others speak with authority
trying to aid. Some say "yes". Some say "no".
Viewpoints stated seem plausible, even if they
do not jive with one another. So it's up to me...
And God.

This life lived has been pliable to the issue
even when doubts arose. Experiences good and
bad. Back and forth. Where the true senses lay...
more than evident. Senses enveloped by guilt.
Shouldn't that be enough to be decisive? Not
so, if you have been down this road. For is the
guilt justified or is it the product of an extremely
literal comprehension? Regardless, it settled
in this conscience and has only brought torment.

So...again, it's up to God and me. I am the
responsible party. No one can speak for me.
It is my life. A life I want to be in accord with
my Maker. Where to go from here? More prayer?
Absolutely. And for now that prayer is "God have
mercy...Thy will be done". Amen.

A New Life

"New Life". Is it reserved as a result of
conversion, enlightenment, or assets acquired?
I think not. At least not this experience.
Then who or what to give regards and credit
for the positive transformation? A change
that has led to enormous and unimaginable
release.

He said "I have come that you may have life.
And have it abundantly." Is this a "given"
when one first believes? Not. Does the
lack of quality living prove one's unfit
spirituality? While in the midst of turmoil
one might make this assumption. All a part
of the curse. Unavoidable despair ensues.

The "demon"...minus horns, tail and pitchfork.
Not necessarily from the world below. In fact,
it came with the body born. Chemicals swirling
abruptly in the brain...out of sync. Invisible to
others until the occurrence of unacceptable,
inappropriate or bizarre actions and decisions.
Then misunderstanding and strife flourishes.
Perplexities for the observer and the plagued.

Enough of the diagnosis. Back to the "New Life".
How? How does one overcome hardships? No
one is immune. The degree is irrelevant. Pain is
pain. Regardless of the cause, suffering of the
living happens. We are not unique...but one only
knows what one knows. So, despite relationships
we all stand alone. Except for the presence of
our Maker. Yet in the while of torment, little
consolation is felt. Sometimes none. Even so
He remains to sustain.

Again...back to "New Life". The horrors have
been made clear. What is this that is positive?
Peace! So long desired. And here it is! Finally!
It was the wait, the wars, the warped, the
wrestling, the wounds. For this one, those
have been "the making" of the peace.
A heavy price paid, enjoyment all the more.
Peace...yes, peace.

There has not been death, but eternity has
already begun. The eternal life which was
promised. Get Back! Surely, I exaggerate!
Problems are still bound. True. But resilience
has been proven. So, in mid-life there is a
"New Life"? Yep. A preview of the blockbuster
"Afterlife". Indeed...Heaven On Earth!!!
Endless gratitude.

Safe And Sound

The darkest night, my friend.
Once lurking in my mind, chaotic fight.
Lack of light not the fear, rather spotlights
that would blind then dim. Now a relaxed
state truly called evening.

Daytime, adventure in the simplest sense.
Circles now straight as a path to follow.
Some bustling without the frantic.
Obstacles usually a feat to accomplish proudly.
The laughter no longer nervous reaction.
As the sun goes down, a settling ending a day
worth lived.

The bout of thought calmed. Decisions recessed
to innocent exercise. The "why" no longer destined
to be a crippling source of contention. Breathing
only to keep the heart beating...not labor to doubt.
Proof to be made, handled with care...lacking the
confusion of identity. And so, reason more sure.

The process of life now safe and sound. Deepening
roots to hold in place the growth. Perfection? No
such thing. Instead, love of life the perfect destiny.
Most days reaching that destination. To hold out
my hand and to hold a hand...my responsibility.
Recognition and unending gratitude to the God
I call mine.

At Last...Not Scared To Live

How to say it? It's a vague depth.
I'm living to live. Not drawing morbid
breath. Why is it wrong to allow life
to happen? What? It's not? And here
I've been fighting it for fifty-five years!

So long trying to digest a person who
screams repulsion. Did I hate myself
that bad? Well, there was one aspect
of my being that did not jive with what
I deemed acceptable.

How to come to terms? A realization.
An awakening. An internalization.
And as I look at my life thus far...
an evolution.

What have I learned? A stumbling block.
A guilt. A worry. A shame. A crippling
evaluation of self, had nothing to do with
the spiritual. Instead, the resulting misery
was caused by false perception and extreme
sensitivity.

So what's the deal? I deserve to feel good.
No longer "settle" or "make do". I deserve
good things. Fun things. Delightful things.
There is no price. There is not a fee. I don't
owe a debt to accept being me.

For now, just absorbing the surrounding aura.
Not totally clear...but very definite. No unnecessary
dwelling or delving. No more calculating.
Just living to live!

"To set heights so lofty would seem radically naïve. Yet life's course has afforded this one a peace not kin to any earthly matter." SJB